trotman

CHOOSING YOUR
GCSEs
& OTHER POST-14 OPTIONS

Alan V... ...h Edition

Choosing your GCSEs and other post-14 options

This tenth edition published in 2007 by Trotman
an imprint of Crimson Publishing,
Westminster House, Kew Road, Richmond,
Surrey TW9 2ND
www.crimsonpublishing.co.uk

© Trotman 2007
Previously published as *How to Choose Your GCSEs* by Trotman and Co Ltd

British Library Cataloguing in Publication Data
A catalogue record for this book is available from the British Library

ISBN 978 1 84455 125 5

Typeset by Newgen Imaging Pvt. Ltd., Chennai, India.
Printed and bound in Great Britain by Bell & Bain Ltd, Glasgow

Contents

About the author

Alan Vincent is an educational consultant who has spent most of his life working in various aspects of careers education and guidance. Initially a languages teacher, he has also worked as head of careers in a secondary school, head of guidance and admissions in a 16–19 consortium, as an education business partnership manager and as a SETPOINT manager (promoting careers in science, technology, engineering and mathematics). He has extensive experience in educational and vocational guidance for young people, particularly those in the 14–19 age range. He is currently General Secretary of the Association for Careers Education and Guidance (ACEG) and also manages a local 14–19 partnership of schools and a college of further education.

He is the author of several books, including *Look Ahead: a Guide to Working in Sport* and *Look Ahead: a Guide to Working Abroad* and articles in a wide range of careers publications.

Introduction

What next? This is a question that in future you will probably ask yourself at many stages of your life, but it's one of the first big questions that you need to ask yourself during your life at school. It will have some effect on your 'career', that is to say your pathway through life, from this point. The decisions you make now could influence what choices you are able to make at age 16, 17, 18 or beyond – the choices of A level (or equivalent), what further education or training course to do, and of an eventual job or career. This book gives you details of the most popular GCSEs and other courses that are likely to be available to you, so that you can make an informed choice. The kinds of questions this book can help you answer include:

- ❯ what GCSEs are available?
- ❯ what are the other Key Stage 4 options?
- ❯ how can I choose between the different courses?
- ❯ which GCSEs do I need to study for my possible post-16 choices?
- ❯ how can I study and revise effectively?
- ❯ what do I learn in specific subjects?
- ❯ how do subject choices affect my career?

Whatever your situation, getting the right answers to the questions listed above is very important: over-hasty decisions at this stage can have significant consequences later on. With the aid of this book, you should be able to navigate your way through the qualifications maze and make the best choices for you. I wish you well for this process.

The main focus in this book is on GCSEs and other courses common to England, Wales and Northern Ireland.

How to use this book

Part One of this book focuses on the different post-14 or Key Stage 4 options available to you. Part Two is a directory of GCSE, vocational and other courses available at this stage of your education. The final part discusses how to make your studies a success and includes information on how exam boards assess GCSE and other courses, with some hints about studying and revising effectively. The End Note explores some of the options open to you with the qualifications you have achieved by age 16.

If you're not sure of the meaning of any of the terms used in the book, you can refer to the Glossary of terms and abbreviations on page 10.

You may already have realised from your experience of studying so far that everybody learns in a different way. In the same way, people read books differently. Some like to read them cover to cover; others prefer to start with the section that seems most relevant to them. You can approach this book in either way. If you need a complete introduction to Key Stage 4 courses, it would be a good idea to read through the book and make a note of any especially important points. If you already have some knowledge but need help with a specific point, the following questionnaire should help point you to the most relevant areas:

	GCSE (or equivalent) issue	**Which section of the book?**
1	I'm not sure whether I ought to concentrate entirely on GCSEs or whether to take at least one applied or vocational course.	See 'What are the options?' and 'Choosing your qualification' in Part One, pages 15 and 31.
2	I need to find out about the different kinds of Key Stage 4 qualification.	See 'What are the options?' and 'Choosing your qualification' in Part One, pages 15 and 31.
3	I can't decide which subjects to take and which to give up. How can I choose?	See 'Choosing your subjects', in Part One, page 35.
4	I know I want to carry on later and take A levels but I'm not sure which GCSEs to take.	See 'Choosing your subjects', in Part One, page 35; and Part Two.
5	I want to improve my effectiveness at studying, revision and taking exams.	See 'Making a success of your studies' in Part Three, page 127.
6	I want to find out details about each GCSE subject.	See Part Two.
7	I want to spend part of my time in a college of further education.	See 'Choosing your qualification' in Part One, page 31; Part Two; and End note: What next?' in Part Three, page 137.
8	I want to find out about GCSE equivalents such as BTEC, NVQs and Apprenticeships.	See 'What are the options?' and 'Choosing your qualification' in Part One, pages 15 and 31.
9	I want to find out which qualifications are best for certain types of study or work post-16.	See 'Choosing your qualification' in Part One, page 31.
10	I want some ideas about what to do after Key Stage 4.	See 'End note: What next?' in Part Three, page 137.

Glossary of terms and abbreviations

Term/abbreviation	Definition
A level	Advanced level
A2	Advanced level – the second half of a full A level
ACEG	Association for Careers Education and Guidance
AEA	Advanced Extension Award
Apprenticeships	A way for young people to train while working in particular skilled areas
AQA	Assessment and Qualifications Alliance
AS level	Advanced Subsidiary Level. Forms the first half of a full A level, but is also a qualification in its own right
ASDAN	Award Scheme Development and Accreditation Network
Bachelor's degrees	The general name for most first degrees in this country (e.g. Bachelor of Arts (BA) or Bachelor of Science (BSc))
BTEC	Business and Technology Education Council (part of Edexcel Foundation)
CACHE	Council for Awards in Childcare and Education
Careers Wales	An all-Wales service that gives people of all ages free careers information, advice and guidance
CCEA	Council for the Curriculum, Examinations and Assessment (Northern Ireland)
CoPE	Certificate of Personal Effectiveness
CRCI	Connexions Resource Centre Index

CV	Curriculum vitae: a summary of your achievements and other details of your life relating to an application for a course or employment
DCSF	Department for Children, Schools and Families
DELLS	Department for Education, Lifelong Learning, and Skills (in Wales)
DfES	Department for Education and Skills (now replaced by the DCSF and DIUS)
Diploma	A new qualification to recognise achievement at ages 14 to 19, combining practical skill development with theoretical and technical understanding and knowledge – sometimes referred to as the Specialised Diploma
DipSW	Diploma in Social Work
DIUS	Department for Innovation, Universities and Skills
EAB	Examinations Appeals Board
Edexcel	One of the main exam boards in England
Fast Tomato	Careers and course information software program
FE	Further education
Field work/field trip	Practical activities related to a subject of study that take place away from school or college, often outdoors, such as a visit to a place of geographical interest
Foundation course	A one-year programme designed to give students the necessary knowledge in a subject to prepare them for higher education. Most common for Art and Design where students need extra time to prepare a portfolio of work to enable them to get into higher education
Foundation degree	This sort of degree lasts two years part-time and is a combination of study and work experience. It can be converted to an Honours degree or used to go on to specific areas of employment
GCE	General Certificate of Education
GCSE	General Certificate of Secondary Education
HNC	Higher National Certificate
HND	Higher National Diploma
IB	International Baccalaureate

ICT	Information and Communications Technology
IGCSE	International GCSE
KS	Key Stage
Kudos Online	Careers information and matching software program (from CASCAiD)
LA	Local Authority
LSC	Learning and Skills Council
NHS	National Health Service
NNEB	National Nursery Examination Board
NVQ	National Vocational Qualification
NQF	National Qualifications Framework
OCR	Oxford, Cambridge and Royal Society of Arts Examining Board
Ofsted	Office for Standards in Education
QCA	Qualifications and Curriculum Authority
RS	Religious Studies
Specialised Diploma	See Diploma (above)
Syllabus	An outline of the course of study produced by exam boards
UCAS	Universities and Colleges Admissions Service
UMS	Uniform Mark Scale (in the assessment of modular GCSEs)
Training providers	These organisations set up work-based training with employers. Some specialise in certain types of training (e.g. Business Administration or IT), while others cover a broader range of occupational areas. Some also provide their own in-house training.
WJEC	Welsh Joint Education Committee
Work-based training	Training in a particular occupational area with an employer in the workplace
Work-related learning	Learning within and outside the curriculum about the world of work

PART ONE: OPTIONS AND DECISIONS

What are the options?

This section covers:
» *an outline of the main Key Stage 4 courses and qualifications.*

Key Stage 4 normally refers to Years 10 and 11 in secondary schools. Traditionally, these are the years when you prepare for examinations taken towards the end of Year 11. However, some of these exam courses now start in Year 9 (sometimes even earlier). Many younger students are following Key Stage 4 courses in one or more subjects. We have therefore chosen to refer to Key Stage 4 rather than 14–16 in this book.

The Key Stage 4 curriculum has changed a great deal in recent years and further changes are still taking place. The government wants to encourage greater freedom and flexibility for schools, so that they can provide a curriculum that meets the needs of all students.
The government wants to:

» get the basics right
» strengthen vocational routes
» ensure the curriculum is sufficiently challenging for all students
» reduce the assessment burden
» prepare young people better for the world of work.

Some of the main features of the reforms affecting Key Stage 4 have been:

» a stronger focus on Mathematics and English
» development of 'functional' English, Mathematics and ICT in GCSE, and basic/key skills
» development of online/when ready tests in functional English and Mathematics.

Other significant changes:

⊛ Design and Technology and Modern Foreign Languages are no longer compulsory for all students.
⊛ schools have to provide the opportunity for students to take a course in each of four 'entitlement areas' – the Arts, Design and Technology, Modern Foreign Languages and the Humanities. This is so that students can take these subjects if they wish to.
⊛ Science is now compulsory.

The statutory curriculum therefore consists of: English, Mathematics, Science, Information and Communications Technology (ICT), Physical Education (PE), Citizenship, Religious Studies (RS), Sex Education, Careers Education, and Work-Related Learning (Work-Related Education in Wales).

Note: an 'approved qualification' is an external qualification that has been approved by the Secretary of State. All such qualifications can be viewed at www.dcsf.gov.uk/section96.

Compulsory subjects

During Key Stage 4 there are some subjects that everyone has to take, but others are optional – you can choose whether to take them or not. All students have to take English, Mathematics, Science and ICT, because they are part of the National Curriculum and because they will help you build up the skills you'll need in the future, such as reading efficiently, writing clearly, being able to use numbers and problem solving. In Wales you must also study Welsh. In addition, everyone has to study Careers Education, Citizenship, Physical Education (PE), Religious Studies, Sex Education and Work-Related Learning/Education. However, you may not have to take exams in these subjects. Some schools have other compulsory subjects. You should check what they are in your school.

GCSEs

The GCSE is still the main way of assessing attainment at the end of compulsory secondary education. You can take GCSEs in nearly 50 different subjects, including eight 'applied' (work-related) subjects.

The GCSE is offered by the awarding bodies, which are independent businesses. There are three main awarding bodies in England: the Assessment and Qualifications Alliance (AQA), Edexcel, and Oxford, Cambridge and RSA Examinations (OCR). Schools are free to choose – from a limited range offered by the exam boards – the GCSE syllabuses they offer. All syllabuses are in line with the National Curriculum programmes of study.

GCSEs mainly involve theoretical study, but there is also some investigative work. In some subjects they also involve some practical work.

All GCSEs must include opportunities for candidates to develop – and be assessed on – the main Key Skills (Communication, Application of Number, Information Technology). These Key Skills are pitched at a level to suit the student. Where appropriate, there are also opportunities for the development and assessment of the 'wider' Key Skills: working with others, improving own learning and performance, and problem solving.

All GCSEs are also expected to make a contribution to aspects of learning that are considered fundamental to the National Curriculum, including:

» environmental issues
» ethical values
» European issues
» health and safety
» spiritual, moral, social and cultural development.

GCSEs are usually assessed by a mixture of coursework and examination, with grades awarded in the range A*–G. The exams are set according to criteria that provide guidance on syllabus content. All GCSE syllabuses must be approved by the Qualifications and Curriculum Authority (QCA). A quality assurance framework ensures that standards are maintained evenly between awarding bodies and syllabuses.

Entries for full GCSEs total 5.75 million per year. Results have continued to improve in recent years, with almost one in five entries in England, Wales and Northern Ireland being awarded the top A* or A grades. In 2006, the proportion getting grade C or above rose 1.2 percentage points from the previous year, to 62.4%, with only 1.9% failing.

Employers regard GCSE as a key factor when looking at young people whom they might employ. When the Learning and Skills Council (LSC) surveyed 412 employers, they found that 15% of them ignored CVs if the job applicant did not have five good GCSEs (usually meaning five at grades A*–C). On average, employers said they would pay someone a starting salary 17% higher if they had five good GCSEs.

Applied GCSEs

Applied GCSEs are each related to a broad area of work, such as business or manufacturing. They are available in the following areas of study:

- Applied Art and Design
- Applied Business
- Applied Information and Communications Technology (ICT)
- Applied Science
- Engineering
- Health and Social Care
- Leisure and Tourism
- Manufacturing.

Other subjects are also becoming available, including Construction and the Built Environment, Applied French, Hospitality and Catering, and Applied Physical Education.

Applied GCSEs are assessed at the same standard as other GCSEs, although the work you produce will have a more practical emphasis. In Applied GCSEs, the focus is mainly on coursework. You will carry out your own investigations and produce a portfolio of work. There are still some tests or exams. The qualification is made up of three units of equal value. Normally, two-thirds of your work is assessed by your teachers, and one third by external examiners. As with other GCSEs, Applied GCSEs are graded A*–G, but each Applied GCSE is equal to two GCSEs.

If you are at school, your lessons for taking an Applied GCSE may take place in a local college or at a vocational learning centre.

Short GCSE courses

The GCSE (Short Course) is designed to take only half the study time of a full GCSE. The short course can be taught over one or two years. In Design and Technology, students must take at least a short course.

GCSE short courses require students to do coursework and exams to the same standards as a full GCSE, but they cover only half the content. GCSE short courses are graded A*–G, and each one counts as half a GCSE. Employers and colleges of further education understand that GCSE short courses are equal to half a GCSE, so that, if you do two short courses, you will have the equivalent of one GCSE.

Short courses are available in:

- Art and Design
- Business Studies
- Design and Technology
- Electronics
- Geography
- History
- Information and Communications Technology
- Modern Foreign Languages
- Music
- Physical Education
- Religious Studies.

They can be used in different ways. For example:

- they can help more able students to take more subjects, such as a second modern foreign language
- if other subject choices prevent a student from taking a full GCSE, they can still gain a short course qualification in subjects such as Art and Design, Geography, ICT, PE or Religious Studies (remember that RS and PE are compulsory subjects, though they don't necessarily require an exam qualification)
- students who need extra time to develop can cover a GCSE (Short Course) in the time taken by a full GCSE course.

Short courses aren't an easy option. Even though they are meant to take up just half the time, they can end up taking more than that.

Diplomas

Diplomas, sometimes referred to as Specialised Diplomas, are the newest qualification offered to the 14–19 age group (including Key Stage 4). Many local 14–19 partnerships (schools, colleges and training organisations) are due to start offering the first Diplomas from September 2008. It is expected that up to 40,000 young people will be taking one of the new Diplomas in the first year.

The new Diplomas will provide an alternative to more traditional education and qualifications. They have been developed by employers, schools, colleges and universities to help young people realise their potential and gain knowledge and skills in a 'real world' environment.

Each Diploma is an all-round package intended to give students the right knowledge, experience, insight and attitude to prepare them for the next stage in their learning or career pathway – at school, college, university or work.

The range of Diplomas available means they are relevant and suitable for all ability levels – the most able students, many of whom will be going on to university courses, as well as for young people who feel that they want to go straight into work after leaving school.

Students will be able to select whichever level Diploma suits them best:

» Level 1: equivalent in size and status to four or five GCSEs at grades D to G.
» Level 2: equivalent in size and status to five or six GCSEs at grades A* to C.
» Level 3: equivalent in size and status to three A levels (a level 3 'progression' Diploma, equivalent in size and status to two A levels, will also be available).

For most young people at Key Stage 4, the Diploma option will be at level 1 or level 2, with progression opportunities to higher-level Diplomas or other options (including A levels, BTECs or Apprenticeships).

In the first year of the offer (2008) courses will be available in these five areas:

» Construction and the Built Environment
» Creative and Media
» Engineering
» Information Technology
» Society, Health and Development.

Local partnerships have had to apply for the right to run these Diploma courses. In each of the learning lines the partnerships have been working with employers to give young people hands-on options alongside other qualifications like GCSEs, A levels and Apprenticeships. Students will be able to learn in different environments, including schools, colleges and the workplace. The new qualifications are intended to help students progress towards skilled jobs and further and university education.

Further areas are due to become available over the next few years, with the following learning lines coming on stream in 2009 and 2010.

From 2009

» Business Administration and Finance
» Hair and Beauty
» Hospitality and Catering
» Land-based and Environmental
» Manufacturing.

From 2010

» Public Services
» Retail
» Science
» Sport and Leisure
» Travel and Tourism.

All the Diplomas will ensure plenty of further study in English, Mathematics, IT, and personal learning and thinking skills. Each Diploma will also include a project aimed at helping develop students' ability in independent work, and every student will have at least 10 days' work experience. Employer involvement in the design and delivery of the Diplomas is an important part of these new qualifications and should ensure that they are valued by employers as a school- or college-leaving qualification, while the higher levels will also be accepted for university entrance.

Work-related learning

It is a statutory requirement that all young people should experience some work-related learning at Key Stage 4. The idea is that all young people need to learn *through* experience of work, to learn *about* work and working practices, and to learn the *skills for* work. All students should be able to benefit from such experience, which may, for example, include enterprise education, work-based experience, or links with careers education or citizenship.

There are two aspects to the requirement for work-related learning. First, schools must provide work-related learning for all students. Second, there is a non-statutory framework that sets out the minimum that schools should provide for all students. It should be possible for schools to deliver the minimum requirement for work-related learning across the curriculum. So you will probably not meet it as a separate subject with its own curriculum time.

How is work-related learning assessed?

Much work-related learning is not formally assessed. However, schools are free to accredit work-related learning and there are a number of qualifications on the QCA approved list. For example, OCR has a range of qualifications, covering both Preparation for Employment and Career Planning (including Job-seeking Skills). These qualifications are offered at entry level and through to level 3. The National Open College Network has both Foundation (level 1) and Intermediate (level 2) awards for Careers Education and Preparation for Working Life, which equate to two GCSEs.

Work experience can also fit into accreditation schemes. For example, preparation for employment qualifications include work experience and are designed to help students develop their workplace skills while also providing an extra qualification.

Entry level qualifications

Entry level is the first level on the National Qualifications Framework. Entry level qualifications are intended for students who are not yet ready to take qualifications in one or more areas of learning at level 1 of the National Qualifications Framework. But they can also be taken in addition to GCSEs and are broadly the same level as the National Curriculum levels 1, 2 and 3.

With entry level qualifications, the focus is on building basic knowledge and skills and gaining the ability to apply learning in everyday situations. Entry level qualifications are not geared towards particular occupations, but can support you in progressing to a GCSE or a level 1 qualification such as an NVQ. Entry level qualifications are available in a wide range of subjects – National Curriculum subjects, vocational subjects, skills for working life, life skills and basic skills. One example is the CACHE Entry Level Certificate in Preparation for Childcare, which is sometimes offered by schools or school–college partnerships.

There are over 100 entry level certificates in all, though there will probably only be a limited choice in your local school, college or partnership. Entry level qualifications available nationally can be grouped into four broad areas:

- core subjects, such as English, Science and Mathematics
- skills areas, including literacy, numeracy and life skills
- general vocational subjects that offer a broad introduction to the world of work
- more specific vocational subjects, including retail, hairdressing and office practice.

If you opt for entry level certificates in National Curriculum subjects at school, they usually take one or two years to complete in Year 10 or Years 10 and 11.

While entry level qualifications can often be studied in further education colleges or at school, they are also available in other community settings.

How are entry level qualifications assessed?

The qualifications – entry level certificates or awards – are graded Entry 1, Entry 2 or Entry 3. They are made up of a number of units, each assessed separately. This means that your achievements are recognised at every step, as you complete each unit. You are assessed by a combination of tests, assignments and practical tasks. Assessment can be of written, oral or practical work. You may also have to produce a portfolio that shows evidence of what you have achieved. The portfolio may contain, for example, witness statements (a written or oral account of your performance), videos, audio material and photographs.
The portfolio is assessed by teachers in your school or learning centre.

Different subjects and courses will vary in structure, content and number of units. When you complete all the units, you get the full certificate.

Entry level and progression pathways

You can progress from one entry level to the next. At Entry 3, the qualifications are designed to help you move on to related qualifications at level 1 of the National Qualifications Framework, such as:

- BTEC introductory or level 1 Awards, Certificates or Diplomas
- GCSEs
- Key Skills
- NVQs
- Skills for Life.

Entry level qualifications can also lead to work-based learning (such as an Apprenticeship) or straight into a job.

Vocational courses

While many of the courses described so far include a significant element of work-related learning, vocational courses put even more emphasis on preparation for working life. At Key Stage 4, such courses are likely to be part of a broader package of more general learning. However, they provide an important alternative for some young people who are ready to take a further step towards preparing themselves for working life, perhaps by learning about, and through, work in a particular occupational area.

It will be difficult for most schools to provide a full range of vocational courses. However, many schools are now working with other partners, particularly further education colleges, to provide a range of vocational learning programmes. These programmes allow some Key Stage 4 students to follow courses not provided at their own school. The courses lead to vocational qualifications, such as GCSEs in vocational subjects or NVQs.

BTEC (Business Technology and Education Council) qualifications

BTEC qualifications are work-related qualifications, available in a wide range of subjects, including:

- Art and Design
- Business
- Construction
- E-Business
- Engineering
- Hair and Beauty
- Health and Social Care
- Hospitality and Catering
- IT and Computing
- Land-based
- Logistics
- Media, Music and Performing Arts
- Public Services
- Retail
- Science
- Sport
- Travel and Tourism.

They provide a practical approach to learning and skills development alongside the necessary theoretical background.

You can take a BTEC qualification if you are interested in learning more about a particular sector or industry. Many of these qualifications have been designed in collaboration with industry, so they can give you the skills and knowledge that employers are looking for. They can be taken either as a way of preparing directly for entry to work or as a step towards continued study at the next level, in a school, college or a more specialist vocational area.

The qualifications offer a mix of theory and practice, and can also include an element of work experience. They can take the form of (or be part of) a technical certificate, one of the key components of an Apprenticeship.

BTEC qualifications range from entry level to level 8 on the National Qualifications Framework.

How are BTEC qualifications assessed?
The main responsibility for assessment in BTEC qualifications usually rests with your teacher or trainer. Depending on the nature and level of the particular qualification, some assessment may also be done by external examiners. You will complete a range of assignments, case studies and practical activities, as well as a portfolio of evidence that shows the work you have done. BTEC qualifications are graded pass, merit or distinction.

OCR Nationals
Like BTEC qualifications, OCR Nationals are work-related qualifications. They are available in the following subjects:

» Business
» Design
» Health and Social Care
» IT
» Media
» Public Services
» Science
» Sport
» Travel and Tourism.

They provide a practical approach to learning and skills development alongside the necessary theoretical background.

You can take an OCR National if you are interested in learning more about a particular sector or industry. Many have been designed in collaboration with industry, so they can equip you with the skills and knowledge that employers are looking for. They can be taken either as a way of preparing for entry to work or as a step towards continued study at the next level, in a school, college or a more specialist vocational area.

The qualifications offer a mix of theory and practice, and can also include an element of work experience. They can take the form of (or be part of) a technical certificate, one of the key components of an Apprenticeship.

OCR Nationals are available at levels 1 to 3. At level 2, for example, they are aimed at enabling students to perform a variety of tasks with some guidance or supervision.

How are OCR Nationals assessed?
The main responsibility for assessment in OCR Nationals rests with your teacher or trainer. Depending on the nature and level of the particular qualification, some assessment may also be done by external examiners. You will complete a range of assignments, case studies and practical activities, as well as a portfolio of evidence that shows the work you have done.

OCR Nationals are graded pass, merit or distinction.

City & Guilds qualifications
City & Guilds is another exam board that provides a wide range of courses, through all NQF levels. Their qualifications are mostly vocational, but they also offer courses in, for example, Literacy, Numeracy and IT. These are sometimes available in schools and more often in colleges and the workplace, or in preparation for employment.

Young Apprenticeships
Young Apprenticeships at Key Stage 4 provide another way of combining continued school study with a taste of real work at college, with a training provider and/or in the workplace. The Young Apprenticeship programme is aimed at able and motivated students who want a more practical style of learning.

Young Apprenticeships may be available in your area in subjects such as:

» Art and Design
» Business Administration
» Construction
» Engineering
» Food and Drink Manufacturing
» Hairdressing
» Health and Social Care
» Hospitality
» Motor Industry
» Performing Arts
» Retail
» Science and the Electricity Industry
» Sports Management, Leadership and Coaching
» Textiles.

You study the normal curriculum at school, including English, Mathematics, ICT and Science.

You spend around two days a week working towards NVQs or other nationally recognised vocational qualifications. This time may be spent at a college of further education, although some schools are also able to provide this part of the programme. You will also spend up to 50 days over two years gaining experience with an employer, training company or college (or a combination of two or three of these).

After completing a Young Apprenticeship you can choose to continue in education and training, or you can go on to do a full-time Apprenticeship in the same sector area. If you have completed the Young Apprenticeship programme you may be able to move more quickly towards completion of a full-time Apprenticeship in your chosen area.

Other vocational qualifications

There are many other vocational courses that schools or colleges offer that are not included in the above categories. Some of them take the form of 'taster' courses, providing a basic introduction to an occupational sector. These tend not to lead to a formal qualification.

ASDAN

The Award Scheme Development and Accreditation Network (ASDAN) is a curriculum development organisation. It is also an awarding body approved by the Department for Children, Schools and Families (DCSF), the Qualifications and Curriculum Authority (QCA), Department for Education, Lifelong Learning and Skills (Wales) (DELLS) and Council for the Curriculum, Examinations and Assessment (Northern Ireland) (CCEA). ASDAN offers a wide range of curriculum programmes and qualifications for all abilities, mainly in the 11–25 age group.

ASDAN programmes and qualifications aim to enrich the curriculum though activity-based programmes. They fit within a framework for the development, assessment and accreditation of Key Skills and other personal and social skills.

ASDAN programmes run in schools include:

- Certificate of Personal Effectiveness (CoPE): levels 1–3 provide a qualification outcome for the ASDAN Silver, Gold and Universities Awards, the FE Awards and the Short Courses Awards.
- Key Skills Qualifications: Improving Own Learning, Working with Others, Problem Solving.

- Certificate in Career Planning (levels 1–3) assists in the development and accreditation of careers-related education and guidance at both Key Stage 4 and post-16.
- The Certificate in Life Skills: a unit-based qualification that offers accreditation at Entry 1, 2 and 3.

National Vocational Qualifications (NVQs)

NVQs are work-related qualifications that focus on the practical skills and knowledge needed to do a job. They are more common post-16, for example as part of an Apprenticeship, but in some cases you can also do an NVQ while you are still at school.

See page 142 for further information on NVQs.

Key Skills and Functional Skills

Key Skills

Whatever subjects or courses you are taking, you will also need the skills that will help you when you start to look for work – and in life more generally. Key Skills are transferable skills: you can use them in different situations. They are the sort of skills that employers see as essential in people they are recruiting. The three main Key Skills are:

- Application of Number
- Communication
- Information and Communications Technology.

There are also three 'wider' Key Skills:

- Improving own Learning and Performance
- Problem Solving
- Working with Others.

You will study and develop these Key Skills at school or college, often as part of another course (see also 'Functional Skills', below). Of course, there is also plenty of opportunity to develop the Key Skills outside the classroom, e.g. through the Duke of Edinburgh's Award Scheme or by getting involved in a club or sporting activity. Later on, after leaving school, you may find that you can take Key Skills qualifications through an employer or training providers. For example, Key Skills are also included in an Apprenticeship. They also form part of some higher education courses.

From your point of view, Key Skills qualifications serve several useful purposes:

◉ they give you firm evidence of what you have achieved in your learning programme
◉ they will help build your confidence in your own abilities
◉ they will support your CV and show employers what you can do
◉ they will help you move on to further qualifications, including higher education (see 'UCAS points' below).

How Key Skills are taught and assessed
Key Skills are available at levels 1–4 of the National Qualifications Framework and there are no minimum entry requirements. You can study them alongside other types of qualification, such as GCSEs, but you do not necessarily take the qualification at the same level as your other qualifications: you take them at whichever level best suits you.

Each Key Skill is assessed separately. The assessment is based on a portfolio you produce and this is assessed internally by your school, college or trainer. The portfolio is a folder of evidence that demonstrates that you have the necessary skills to pass.

For the three main Key Skills, you also take a test, which is marked externally by an awarding body. At levels 1 and 2, the test consists of 40 multiple choice questions, each with four possible answers. If you don't pass the test, you can normally retake it as many times as you want. However, you would need to check these arrangements with your school, college or learning provider.

You can also take a practice test online for the three main Key Skills qualifications at the Key Skills website: www.keyskills4u.com.

UCAS points
All six Key Skills attract points on the 'UCAS Tariff' for entry into higher education. From 2007 entry onwards, the three wider Key Skills will also earn UCAS points. The points you get for each Key Skill depend on the level of qualification you pass:

◉ level 2 is rewarded with 10 UCAS points
◉ level 3 is rewarded with 20 UCAS points
◉ level 4 is rewarded with 30 UCAS points.

Functional Skills

Functional Skills are intended to help young people communicate more effectively and to be literate in the broadest sense of the word. They help learners make sense of their community and the wider world and develop their own perspectives. With good Functional Skills, you should also be able to respond more effectively to changes in technology and everyday life. Functional Skills promote the key concepts of 'competence' and 'critical understanding'.

As part of the phased implementation of Functional Skills, a pilot for GCSE candidates was due to run from September 2007 for two years in English and ICT and for three years in Mathematics. This pilot will include those schools and colleges involved in the first phase of the introduction of the new Diplomas (see page 19). Schools, colleges and training providers are currently being encouraged to prepare for the introduction of Functional Skills. Their preparation is intended to be built on the lessons from existing good practice in GCSE and Key Skills.

How to find out more about each type of qualification

- BTEC: www.btec.org.uk
- entry level qualifications: www.dcsf.gov.uk/qualifications/
- GCSEs, Applied GCSEs and Short GCSEs: see Part Two of this book
- NVQs: www.qca.org.uk/14-19/qualifications/
- other vocationally related qualifications: www.qca.org.uk/14-19/ qualifications/
- Young Apprenticeships – www.apprenticeships.org.uk/

By now you should have an idea of some of the most common Key Stage 4 options. But how do you decide between them? The following pages will help.

Choosing your qualification

In this section you will:
- » *get help with choosing the right Key Stage 4 qualifications*
- » *find out how the different qualifications compare to one another in terms of status*
- » *do a brief exercise to help you choose the right qualifications.*

There are so many different options available at Key Stage 4 that it can seem rather confusing. So how do you set about making the best choice? One of the best ways is by comparing qualifications with one another and by really focusing on what it is that you think you might do afterwards. Let's start by comparing the qualifications with one another.

One of the reasons why the government introduced the National Qualifications Framework (NQF) is to make it easier to compare the various qualifications. The different qualifications are grouped at nine different levels (entry level and levels 1 to 8). All qualifications approved by QCA on behalf of the government are allocated to a certain level. This means that they can be compared with each other and so that learners can see how to progress from one level to the next.

Qualifications at the same level in the NQF all recognise a similar level of knowledge, skills and understanding, although the subjects studied may be quite different. The higher the level, the more advanced the qualification and the more knowledge and skill it requires.

Look at the chart below to find out how different qualifications compare. You will see, for example, that GCSEs cover the Foundation and Intermediate levels (levels 1 and 2). Grades D–G are level 1 and grades A*–C are level 2. A levels are level 3 qualifications.

Qualification level	What it means	Examples of qualifications at this level
Entry level	Builds a basic level of knowledge, understanding and skills and is not geared towards specific occupations.	Entry 1, Entry 2 and Entry 3, in a range of areas including National Curriculum subjects, life skills, basic skills and skills for working life.
Level 1	Basic knowledge, understanding and skills, and the ability to apply learning to everyday situations. In some cases, may include initial preparation for job competence.	GCSE grades D–G; ASDAN level 1 certificates; Key Skills level 1; VRQ level 1, e.g. OCR Nationals, BTEC Introductory; NVQ level 1.
Level 2	Basic knowledge and/or skills in relation to subject or sector areas; gaining ability to apply learning to a varied range of tasks. This is normally the minimum level required by employers and is critical to going on to further study and higher-level skills.	GCSE grades A*–C; Key Skills level 2, VRQ level 2, e.g. City & Guilds Progression awards; NVQ level 2.
Level 3	Learning at this level involves obtaining in-depth knowledge, understanding and skills, and a higher level of application. Appropriate for people who want to go to university, do further training or enter employment.	GCE AS and A levels, Advanced Extension Awards, Key Skills level 3, VRQ level 3, e.g. NVQ level 3.

Qualification level	What it means	Examples of qualifications at this level
Level 4–8	Specialist learning involving high level of knowledge in a specific occupational role or study. Appropriate for people working or wishing to progress to specialised technical and professional jobs, and/or managing and developing others.	Certificates and Diplomas of Higher Education, bachelor's degrees, Foundation degrees, HNCs and HNDs, Key Skills level 4, NVQ levels 4 and 5.

If you are still having difficulty deciding which is the most appropriate set of qualifications for you, the following exercise should help. Look at the statement on the left-hand side and see if it applies to you. If it does, then look at the corresponding qualification(s) on the right-hand side. Then you can research these particular qualifications further, through this book and elsewhere.

Does this statement apply to you?	Most appropriate qualification(s)
I want a qualification that will give me practical skills towards a specific job.	Young Apprenticeships; NVQs; BTEC qualifications and OCR Nationals. All probably with some GCSEs.
I want an academic qualification that will help me go on to A levels (or equivalent).	GCSEs; Applied GCSEs; Diplomas.
I want to carry on with full-time study at 16+, but on a course related to a particular sector of work.	Diplomas; GCSEs; Applied GCSEs.
I think I might struggle to achieve any sort of grades at GCSE.	Entry level. But you may be able to mix this with some GCSE study.
I am quite good at academic work, but enjoy practical work more.	Applied GCSEs; Diplomas; Young Apprenticeships.
I've got so many subjects I want to take and am reluctant to give them all up.	GCSEs and Short Course GCSEs.

The next section focuses on choosing between specific subjects, mainly with GCSEs in mind. If you need more specific information on other Key Stage 4 qualifications, look at the relevant websites listed on page 30.

Choosing your subjects

This section includes:
- » **answers to the most common questions asked by prospective students**
- » **exercises to help you decide between subjects**
- » **a breakdown of the GCSE results from summer 2006**
- » **sources of further information.**

This section looks at the kinds of things to consider when you're trying to choose between different subjects: this is one of the dilemmas that students face when thinking about their Key Stage 4 options. These are some of the most common questions that young people ask.

Should I choose those subjects I am strongest in?

On the whole, this is as good a reason as any to choose a subject at GCSE, for example. If you are strong in a particular subject that you have already been studying, it is more than likely that you will do well at Key Stage 4. This means that you should achieve a good grade at GCSE. It also keeps open higher-level study in these same subjects, at A level and beyond. Remember, though, that it is important to structure a well-balanced programme of study at Key Stage 4. You may even find that it is in your best long-term interests to keep up one or more subjects where you do not feel as strong. For example, if you are very good at Biology and have an interest in an eventual career in the biological sciences, you will need to keep up Chemistry (by taking it as a separate GCSE or within GCSE Science); this might apply even if you feel at present that you might struggle to achieve the standard required in Chemistry.

Should I choose those subjects I enjoy the most?

It's possible to be good at a subject and yet not really enjoy it – and the reverse can also be true. However, people who opt for subjects they are really interested in tend to do better in those subjects. This is largely because they have a natural talent for that area, but also because they are likely to have the motivation to do the additional study that is needed to get the top grades.

If you are struggling to think about what your natural talents are, the following table might help you. Look at the skills on the left-hand side of the table and decide which ones you'd definitely like to use in further study, and those you definitely wouldn't be interested in acquiring. Put a tick or a cross in each case. Then look to see which subjects match which skills and see if that sheds any light on where your natural talents lie.

Type of skill	I like using this skill	I hate using this skill	Subjects that require this skill a lot
Communication skills (good at communicating, reading, writing essays, learning languages)			All subjects, but especially English (compulsory), Health and Social Care, History, Social Science subjects, Leisure and Tourism, Modern Foreign Languages
Attention to detail (being good with small details, checking facts, figures, specifics, quantities)			All science subjects, as well as Geography, Health and Social Care, History, Construction, Engineering, Manufacturing
Physical ability (e.g. making things, doing things, exercising, using your hands, doing experiments)			Physical Education, science subjects, Engineering, Art and Design, Design and Technology, Manufacturing
Creative ability (e.g. making things, writing or drawing, performing)			Art and Design, Design and Technology, English (compulsory) and English Literature, Drama, Performing Arts, Music

Type of skill	I like using this skill	I hate using this skill	Subjects that require this skill a lot
Memory and recall skills (memorising facts, words, vocabulary and theories)			Many subjects, but especially History, Mathematics (compulsory), science subjects, Modern Foreign Languages
IT and computing skills (using hardware, software and systems)			ICT (compulsory), Design and Technology, Engineering, Leisure and Tourism, Physics
Mathematical skills (using figures and statistics to conclude and investigate things; doing mental calculations)			Mathematics (compulsory), all science subjects (especially Physics), Engineering, Design and Technology, Geography
Emotional intelligence skills (empathising, intuition, vision, creativity, tact, interpersonal skills)			Religious Studies, English (compulsory) and English Literature, Health and Social Care, History, Leisure and Tourism, Music
Spatial awareness and mechanical skills (being able to 'see' what shapes will fit where; making and working with mechanical objects)			Engineering, Physics, Art and Design, Design and Technology, ICT (compulsory), Construction

Type of skill	I like using this skill	I hate using this skill	Subjects that require this skill a lot
Business skills (understanding business, finance and economics, as well as specific sectors of work)			Business Studies, Leisure and Tourism, Retail
Citizenship skills (being familiar with and learning about social, political and environmental issues of the past and present)			Citizenship (compulsory), Geography, History, Social Science subjects, Religious Studies, English (compulsory), English Literature

How are the different subjects assessed?

Most GCSEs and their equivalents are assessed by a combination of written exams (either during or at the end of your course), coursework (essays, projects or case studies) – completed during the course, usually in your own time – and practical exams. Not only are there variations between subjects in the type of assessment, but there will also be some variation between different examination boards offering the same subject. So try to work out whether you are better at exams, coursework or practical work and bear that in mind when choosing your subjects.

How can I avoid taking too many exams?

Many of the subjects you'll study in Key Stage 4 will be assessed on a mixture of coursework and exams. Coursework is a useful way of showing what you can do, especially when an exam is not appropriate (for example, a music presentation). The coursework element of a subject can make up a significant proportion of your final mark – for some subjects, coursework counts for more than half of the total. The detailed entries for each subject in Part Two will give you some idea of the assessment weighting – how many of the marks are given for coursework and how many for the examination component.

However, even if you do prefer coursework to exam assessment, be wary of coursework overload – don't overburden yourself with coursework.

Some subjects, History and Geography, for example, involve more research-based coursework to be done outside the classroom, while Mathematics and Modern Foreign Languages, on the other hand, probably include relatively little. As it is important to make sure you have enough time to do every project well, make sure you get the workload right by *not* picking too many subjects that are heavy on coursework. Check coursework content with your teachers.

You will be doing some coursework throughout your GCSE studies. It will be up to your teachers and the way they organise teaching and learning as to when exactly you do that coursework. Since the coursework marks count towards final grades, you need to take it seriously and do it as well as you can. Try to be well organised and don't leave assignments until the last minute.

Within the individual subject, it is unlikely that you will have any freedom of choice. It is your school that chooses a syllabus from one of the exam boards for each subject. This means that you could be using different exam boards for different subjects, but the most important thing is that you know what work you will be covering in your particular syllabus. Your teacher will make sure you know about this, or you can find it on the relevant exam board website.

What are modular courses?

Some courses have 'modular' options. A modular course is split into different units, with a test or exam at the end of each unit. This means that you sit exams throughout your course instead of doing all the exams at the end of the one- or two-year course. This gives you the opportunity to study relatively small parts of the curriculum in a concentrated period. Each unit or module contains very specific and easily understood learning targets, and learning is assessed at the end of each module.

The different structure of modular courses, with a strong emphasis on assessment and systematic feedback between teacher and student, suits some students better than the more traditional structure. One advantage is that, if you take a modular exam and don't do as well as you expected, you can resit the module to try to improve your grade. The better mark from the two sittings will count towards your final GCSE grade. This is not an easy way out and you still need to work hard on your first attempt. You would also need to speak to your teachers about the arrangements for resitting modules, as these vary depending on the particular course you are studying.

With modular schemes, end-of-unit tests or exams that count towards the final assessment are set and marked externally; and any marks allocated for coursework will be set at the same limit as for the ordinary GCSE in that subject.

If you take any modular exams your results slip may have a 'UMS' (Uniform Mark Scale) mark. UMS is the system that exam boards use to combine different modular marks to get your overall GCSE grade. Your subject teacher or exam officer will be able to tell you more about the UMS system.

Which subjects are necessary if I want to go on to higher education?

Although university may seem a long way off at this stage, there are some choices you make now that could influence the range of courses open to you post-18. For example, some English Literature departments still either insist on, or at least prefer, at least one Modern Foreign Language GCSE. To study a Modern Foreign Language at university, it is an advantage to have studied at least two foreign languages to GCSE level and, if at all possible, beyond. And for degree courses in Dentistry, Medicine and Veterinary Science, you should think seriously about taking all three science subjects separately, or at least GCSE Science *and* GCSE Additional Science.

The problem is that the subjects you need will clearly depend on what you eventually choose to study at university – but you may well not yet know which subject you will want to read at that stage. In most cases, it is expected that you have an A level or equivalent with a good grade in that subject; and this very often (but not always) means that you should take a GCSE in that same subject.

Do I need a GCSE in a subject to do it at A level?

Not necessarily. If you can convince your sixth-form tutors or teachers that you have the right attitude and the potential to do well, then it is possible in some cases to take an A level in a subject you haven't done at GCSE. However, there are clearly some subjects that really build on the knowledge that you will have learned at GCSE. These include:

- Geography
- Mathematics
- Modern Foreign Languages
- Sciences.

It would be difficult to pick these subjects up at A level without any of the building blocks. There are, however, subjects that are often not taught or studied in a secondary school at GCSE level, which most people therefore meet for the first time at A level and which assume no prior knowledge. These include:

- Government and Politics
- Law
- Philosophy
- Sociology.

How do I make sure that my choice of subjects will be in line with my hopes for a career?

Even if you think you know what sort of job or career pathway you want, you should be prepared to research your job ideas more generally and find out which qualifications you will need. You can do this at your school's Connexions or careers resource centre or library, or at your local Connexions or careers centre (your careers teacher will be able to tell you where this is).

If you've no idea at this stage, don't worry. You are probably in the majority ... 13 or 14 is rather early for most people to decide on a career. Your aim now should be to choose a selection of subjects that will keep as many career doors open as possible. There are a few ideas on types of job that link with particular subjects towards the end of each subject entry in Part Two.

Which GCSEs are easiest to get good grades in?

This depends on what you are best at and what you enjoy – that's probably how you will get the best grades. However, every year figures are produced on the GCSE results by the Joint Council for Qualifications. The results for summer 2006 are given below. Be careful, though: do not use the table as an indication of the level of difficulty of a subject and base your choice on that, as there will be many contributing factors as to why one subject gains more top grades than another.

Subject	Gender	Number sat	% of total no. sat	Percentage by grade								
				A*	A	B	C	D	E	F	G	U
Art	Male	86,035	3.0	3.9	9.9	17.2	29.5	16.7	12.2	7.1	3.0	0.5
	Female	126,322	4.3	8.8	18.9	23.8	27.5	11.1	6.1	2.6	1.0	0.2
	All	212,357	3.7	6.8	15.3	21.1	28.3	13.4	8.5	4.5	1.8	0.3
Business Studies	Male	51,452	1.8	4.1	10.5	15.5	28.3	19.1	10.5	5.5	2.9	3.6
	Female	37,905	1.3	5.4	11.7	16.3	29.3	18.8	9.3	4.7	2.1	2.4
	All	89,357	1.6	4.6	11.1	15.8	28.7	19.0	10.0	5.1	2.6	3.1
Design and Technology	Male	203,118	7.2	2.7	9.2	14.2	25.4	21.4	12.4	7.1	3.8	3.8
	Female	168,554	2.2	5.6	17.2	18.6	25.7	16.9	7.9	4.0	2.1	2.0
	All	371,672	1.8	4.0	12.9	16.1	25.6	19.3	10.4	5.7	3.0	3.0
English	Male	362,007	12.7	2.7	8.9	17.0	26.1	21.7	12.6	6.4	2.8	1.8
	Female	359,755	12.4	5.0	13.9	21.8	27.9	18.2	7.9	3.0	1.3	1.0
	All	721,762	12.5	3.9	11.3	19.4	27.0	20.0	10.2	4.8	2.0	1.4
English Literature	Male	275,845	9.7	3.5	11.8	20.7	25.3	17.5	10.9	6.5	2.5	2.3
	Female	296,316	10.2	6.0	17.6	25.3	25.0	14.0	6.9	2.8	1.1	1.3
	All	572,161	9.9	4.8	14.8	23.1	25.1	15.7	8.9	4.1	1.7	1.8
French	Male	104,825	3.7	7.9	11.1	15.8	23.7	19.4	11.7	6.4	3.2	0.8
	Female	131,364	4.5	10.9	14.9	19.3	24.5	16.1	8.1	4.0	1.3	0.4
	All	236,189	4.1	9.6	13.2	17.7	24.2	17.5	9.7	5.1	2.4	0.6
Geography	Male	118,849	4.2	7.6	13.4	16.7	25.3	16.5	9.4	5.5	2.9	2.7
	Female	94,620	3.2	11.2	16.8	18.2	23.3	13.8	7.9	4.3	2.4	2.1
	All	213,469	3.7	9.2	14.9	17.4	24.4	15.3	8.7	5.0	2.7	2.4
German	Male	42,567	1.5	7.2	11.9	17.0	27.6	18.7	9.3	5.2	2.5	0.6
	Female	47,744	1.6	9.8	15.8	20.4	28.3	14.9	6.3	3.0	1.2	0.3
	All	90,311	1.6	8.6	13.9	18.8	28.0	16.7	7.7	4.0	1.9	0.4
History	Male	118,082	4.2	8.6	17.0	19.7	18.5	13.4	9.6	6.7	3.8	2.7
	Female	113,575	3.9	12.0	19.6	20.4	17.4	12.3	8.6	5.2	2.8	1.7
	All	231,657	4.0	10.3	18.2	20.1	18.0	12.8	9.1	6.0	3.3	2.2

ICT	Male	60,888	2.1	4.9	12.4	17.4	23.9	15.6	9.8	7.0	4.4	4.6
	Female	48,713	1.7	7.1	16.2	19.7	23.6	13.8	7.9	5.3	3.1	3.3
	All	109,601	1.9	5.9	14.0	18.5	23.8	14.7	9.0	6.2	3.9	4.0
Mathematics	Male	371,875	13.1	4.2	9.0	17.0	23.3	17.6	13.5	7.9	3.5	4.0
	Female	378,695	13.0	4.1	9.1	18.2	23.6	18.7	13.0	6.8	2.9	3.6
	All	750,570	13.0	4.2	9.0	17.6	23.5	18.1	13.3	7.3	3.2	3.8
Music	Male	31,048	1.1	8.2	18.1	23.6	20.1	11.8	7.9	4.7	2.8	2.8
	Female	29,620	1.0	11.1	22.6	24.4	18.8	9.9	6.0	3.5	1.8	1.9
	All	60,668	1.1	9.6	20.3	24.0	19.5	10.8	7.0	4.1	2.4	2.3
Physical Education	Male	99,614	3.5	4.7	13.4	20.6	21.6	24.6	10.5	3.3	1.0	0.3
	Female	53,212	1.8	8.5	15.3	19.9	19.4	22.4	10.0	3.3	1.0	0.2
	All	152,826	2.7	6.1	14.0	20.3	20.9	23.8	10.3	3.3	1.0	0.3
Religious Studies	Male	69,184	2.4	8.0	16.0	19.9	19.9	14.1	9.5	6.1	3.8	2.7
	Female	90,497	3.1	13.6	21.8	22.4	18.0	10.7	6.5	3.7	2.0	1.3
	All	159,681	2.8	11.2	19.3	21.3	18.8	12.2	7.8	4.7	2.8	1.9
Science: Biology	Male	33,717	1.2	16.9	26.2	26.6	19.7	7.2	1.9	0.7	0.3	0.5
	Female	26,365	0.9	19.7	25.9	23.3	18.1	8.3	2.4	1.0	0.5	0.8
	All	60,082	1.0	18.1	26.1	25.2	19.0	7.6	2.2	0.8	0.3	0.7
Science: Chemistry	Male	32,800	1.2	19.1	25.5	25.5	20.1	6.8	1.9	0.4	0.2	0.5
	Female	23,964	0.8	21.4	25.7	24.3	18.7	6.9	1.9	0.5	0.2	0.4
	All	56,764	1.0	20.1	25.6	24.9	19.6	6.8	1.9	0.4	0.2	0.5
Science: Physics	Male	33,031	1.2	21.6	25.7	24.2	19.6	6.5	1.5	0.4	0.1	0.4
	Female	23,004	0.8	19.4	26.7	24.0	19.8	7.4	1.8	0.4	0.1	0.4
	All	56,035	1.0	20.7	26.1	24.1	19.7	6.9	1.6	0.4	0.1	0.4
Spanish	Male	25,287	0.9	12.7	14.5	15.6	20.8	16.7	10.1	5.8	3.0	0.8
	Female	36,856	1.3	16.3	18.2	17.9	20.7	14.4	7.1	3.5	1.5	0.4
	All	62,143	1.1	14.8	16.7	17.0	20.7	15.4	8.3	4.4	2.2	0.5

For more information about GCSE results from last year, visit www.jcq.org.uk.

How can I find out more?

You will almost certainly need more information and help than this book can give you in making your choices. It's worth remembering that there are many sources of help. Some of these are listed below.

» Careers advisers or personal advisers. If you need additional help to decide on your subject choices, or want to talk about your career options, you can ask for an interview with a careers adviser or personal adviser. These people may not always know you well, but they do have a lot of knowledge about the world of work and the significance of different qualifications for various jobs and careers. They may also organise group talks in your school about specific types of career or on topics related to careers. Your careers adviser or personal adviser is also likely to attend any relevant parents' evenings and any special careers events that relate to Key Stage 4 choices in your school.
» Work experience. Any work experience placement that you take on during Key Stage 4 will give you a taste of the world of work. Even if you are not trying out the sort of career that is of direct interest to you, you will pick up plenty of experience that will help you see where Key Stage 4 choices fit into the business of setting up a career progression pathway for yourself.
» School careers or Connexions library. Your school will have a careers or Connexions library with details on careers, courses and subjects. You should explore the full range of books, leaflets and careers software available in your school.
» Careers or Connexions centre. There will also be a more extensive careers library at your local careers or Connexions centre. These centres are usually located in or near town centres and are open Monday to Friday, including the school holidays. Your careers teacher or co-ordinator will be able to tell you where your nearest centre is and you will be welcome to call in.
» Careers software programs, including Fast Tomato, Kudos.
» Open days at colleges or training providers.
» Careers teacher or co-ordinator.
» Tutors.
» Subject teachers.

Your teachers will see it as part of their responsibility to see that you are entered for the most appropriate subjects and syllabuses available. So, before opting for or committing yourself to, any course, be sure to ask your subject teacher the key questions:

» how much reading is involved?
» how much writing is involved?

- how much coursework is involved?
- what percentage of the marks is given for coursework?
- is there the option of different tiers of assessment (see page 133)?
- is there an oral test?
- will you have to gather information for yourself?
- are there any projects involved?
- what practical skills are involved?
- how much laboratory or fieldwork is involved?

With this information, you should be well placed to begin to make your subject decisions.

Useful websites

Although it cannot replace the value of face-to-face guidance from someone who can respond to your needs and questions, the internet is a fantastic source of information – on both courses and careers.

The QCA has a dedicated 14–19 learning section on its website (www.qca.org.uk/14-19). As well as giving support and guidance to schools and colleges in managing the whole 14–19 phase of education, it aims to help students get the best from their experience of the phase. There are special sections of the website for students and their parents. Other relevant websites:

- Careers Scotland: www.careers-scotland.org.uk
- Careers Service Northern Ireland: www.careersserviceni.com
- Careers Wales: www.careerswales.com
- Connexions Services: www.connexions.gov.uk and www.connexions-direct.com/jobs4u
- Digitalbrain: www.digitalbrain.com

By now you should have plenty of information about what to consider when choosing your subjects. Once you've come up with a shortlist, go to Part Two to look at the relevant subjects in detail. This should confirm your choice, or it may make you reconsider. Either way, it's essential information before you make your final decision.

PART TWO: DIRECTORY OF GCSEs, DIPLOMAS, VOCATIONAL AND OTHER COURSES AVAILABLE 14–16

How to use the directory

What follows is a directory of GCSE subjects. It includes detailed descriptions of all the main subjects that are taken by students at Key Stage 4.

Each subject is covered under the following sections:

» overview of the subject area
» main elements of the course
» applied courses, short courses or other variations available
» how it is taught and assessed
» the subject at A level (or equivalent)
» the subject and choosing a career pathway.

Syllabus information
If you need more information on any subject that interests you, it's a good idea to check out the syllabus of the relevant exam board that your school or college runs. These can be found on the exam board websites listed below.

AS/A levels and equivalents
A levels remain the principal progression route for those wanting to go on to university and/or high-status careers. There are some excellent alternatives, such as the International Baccalaureate (offered by some schools and sixth-form colleges) and BTEC Nationals (usually offered in colleges of further education).

The availability of courses in the subject area at A level and BTEC National is listed in each subject section.

Future careers

Each subject area includes ideas for possible future careers.

What to do next

As you browse the directory, try to have in mind the following questions.

- Would I enjoy studying this?
- Would I do well in the subject, given the type of assessment methods used?
- How would choosing this subject affect my plans for further study ay 16+?
- How would choosing this subject affect my career options?

Then come up with a shortlist of subjects and if you are still finding it difficult to choose between a few subjects, look back at 'Choosing your subjects' in Part One, page 35.

Useful contacts and sources of further information

Regulatory bodies

Each country has a regulatory body for qualifications, which oversees what the exam boards do. Part of their job is to monitor and ensure the consistency of standards.

In England, the regulatory authority is the Qualifications and Curriculum Authority:

Qualifications and Curriculum Authority
QCA Customer Relations
83 Piccadilly
London W1 8QA
Tel: 020 7509 5556
Web: www.qca.org.uk

Wales has the Department for Education, Lifelong Learning and Skills (DELLS). Its regulatory section can be contacted at:
Qualifications and Curriculum Group
Castle Buildings
Womanby Street
Cardiff CF10 1SX
Tel: 029 2037 5400
Web: accac.org.uk

In Northern Ireland the regulatory authority is the Council for the Curriculum, Examinations and Assessments (CCEA):

CCEA
29 Clarendon Road
Clarendon Dock
Belfast BT1 3BG
Tel: 028 9026 1200
Web: www.ccea.org.uk

Exam boards

AQA
Stag Hill House
Guildford
Surrey GU2 7XJ
Tel: 01483 506506
Web: www.aqa.org.uk

ASDAN
Wainbrook House
Hudds Vale Road
St George
Bristol BS5 7HY
Tel: 0117 941 1126
Web: www.asdan.org.uk

Edexcel
190 High Holborn
London WC1V 7BH
Tel: 0870 240980
Web: www.edexcel.org.uk

OCR
9 Hills Road
Cambridge CB2 1PB
Tel: 01223 553311
Web: www.ocr.org.uk

WJEC
245 Western Avenue
Cardiff CF5 2TX
Tel: 029 2026 5000
Web: www.wjec.co.uk

Art and Design

This subject gives students the opportunities to develop:

- creative and imaginative powers, and the practical skills for communicating and expressing ideas, feelings and meanings in art, craft and design
- investigative, analytical, experimental and interpretative capabilities, aesthetic understanding and critical skills
- understanding of codes and conventions of art, craft and design and awareness of contexts in which they operate
- knowledge and understanding of art, craft and design in contemporary societies and in other times and cultures.

GCSE Art and Design

This is an attractive option for students with good basic drawing skills who are interested in developing their visual appreciation of the world around them. Students are given a broad introduction to a wide range of art media and have the opportunity to explore their creative potential in these media.

Main elements of the course

The outline below is based on what the majority of exam board syllabuses include. For an exact definition of the syllabus you will be studying, you should consult your school or the exam board itself.

The course includes integrated critical, practical and theoretical study of drawing, painting and other media (this may include ceramics, collage, photography, printmaking, sculpture and mixed media). There will be some first-hand experience of creating original work. Students are expected to develop knowledge and understanding of:

» how ideas, feelings and meanings are conveyed in images and artefacts
» a range of art, craft and design processes in two and/or three dimensions (*in Northern Ireland, students are required to cover work in both two and three dimensions*), including, where appropriate, the use of computers and ICT
» how images and artefacts relate to their social, historical and cultural context
» a variety of approaches, methods and intentions and the contribution of contemporary practitioners and others from different times and cultures to continuity and change in art, craft and design.

Alternatively, some schools offer specialist options within Art and Design, such as Critical and Contextual Studies, Fine Art, Graphic Design, Photography, Textiles, and 3D Design. Each of these courses can be run at full GCSE level, i.e. as a single GCSE in its own right.

Short course in Art and Design
There is also a short course GCSE available in this subject. The main difference is that the course takes half the time allocated to a full GCSE. Students take on perhaps only one piece of coursework and are awarded only half a GCSE qualification at the end of the course.

See also the introduction to short courses on page 18.

GCSE Applied Art and Design
Applied Art and Design (offered by Edexcel) is equivalent to two GCSEs and is normally allocated twice the time given to a single GCSE. So it will probably take up two of the 'option blocks'. This makes it even more important that students have good basic drawing skills and are well motivated in their study of the subject.

The course is made up of three units of work – 2D and 3D Visual Language; Materials, Techniques and Technology; and Working to Project Briefs.

How is Art and Design taught and assessed?
Art and Design is one of the subject areas where there is a strong practical focus, alongside the 'academic' elements (which include detailed study of particular artists and their work). Students are taught how to critically appraise their own work and that of professional artists.

They learn how to record their observations, experiences and ideas. They develop and explore ideas and learn how to present a personal response to the range of stimuli that art, craft and design media provide. Most schools ensure that students have the opportunity to visit art galleries and exhibitions and meet professional artists, sometimes working with 'artists in residence'.

Because of the dual emphasis on practical and theoretical work, the GCSEs feature coursework as well as an exam. Coursework accounts for 60% and the examination 40% (while in the Applied course it is two-thirds coursework and one-third examination). Students build up a coursework portfolio (usually in the form of a sketchbook, but often including larger pieces of work). The portfolio is based on two, three or four projects for the full course, depending on the exam board. Your teacher will decide which unit topics are selected, but each should be aimed at developing the student's skills, imagination and confidence. The coursework is done both in the classroom and through homework.

For the final project, taken in the final term of Year 11, students have 4–10 weeks (again, depending on the exam board) to prepare their research and thinking and a period of ten hours (spread over two or more days) under exam conditions to complete the piece of work.

The subject at A level
A level courses are available in Art and Design and in Applied Art and Design. These courses have painting and drawing as their main focus, but there are many additional aspects of the course, including:

» 3D design
» fashion and textiles
» fine art
» graphic design
» photography and multimedia
» preparing and working to a brief.

Art and Design and choosing a career pathway
Job opportunities at age 16 are relatively limited in this area of work, but the 14–19 learning stage gives young people interested in art and design the opportunities to experiment with, and develop, their abilities across a spectrum of art and design activity. This is often a narrowing down process, with the option to specialise as you progress. You can explore work-based training (Apprenticeships in England, Modern Apprenticeships in Wales, or Skillseekers and Modern Apprenticeships in Scotland). Or you can stay on at school or college, to study for City & Guilds or

BTEC qualifications in Art and Design or in a related area such as Ceramics, Photography or Textiles.

If you want to continue your studies further at university, most students take a diagnostic one-year foundation course before they go on to start a degree course. These foundation courses are designed to introduce students to a broader range of art and design disciplines and techniques than can usually be offered in a secondary school or college. They are very helpful in enabling students to identify a particular specialism that they want to study in greater depth. However, it is not obligatory to take a foundation course and direct entry to university courses in Art and Design is possible if a student can demonstrate exceptional ability or experience.

Not all Art and Design graduates enter careers in which they make direct use of their artistic ability and training. Perhaps only a quarter end up working as artists or designers, and the proportion is lower still when one looks at those who continue with fine art studies. One growth area in recent years has been in website design, which has some scope for creative and imaginative artists and designers with good IT competence. There are vacancies for graphic design graduates in advertising, the leisure industry, publishing and design consultancy. Many fashion and textiles graduates find jobs in buying and merchandising or with mass production designers. With many of the 3D options (e.g. jewellery and silversmithing, glass and ceramics), it is often most practical to think in terms of self-employment, with consequent implications for business skills and entrepreneurial skills.

Further information

Artcyclopedia: www.artcyclopedia.com

The Artist's Toolkit: www.artsconnected.org/toolkit/index.html

BBC Arts: www.bbc.co.uk/arts; www.bbc.co.uk/blast/art/; www.bbc. co.uk/arts/powerofart/

British Council Arts: www.britishcouncil.org/arts

Design Council: www.designcouncil.org.uk/ and www.yourcreativefuture. org.uk

History of Art: www.besthistorysites.net/arthistory

Institute of Conservation: www.icon.org.uk

National Electronic and Video Archive of the Crafts: www.media.uwe.ac. uk/nevac/

The Art & Design Directory 2007, Trotman

Caprez, Emma Art & Design Uncovered, Trotman

Biology

Biology includes the study of topics such as digestion and nutrition, ecology, evolution, gene technology, microbes, plants, photosynthesis, and respiration and breathing.

GCSE Biology

GCSE Biology is one of three separate science awards (the others are Chemistry and Physics) that together cover the requirements of the Key Stage 4 programme of study. You can also combine the study of these three subjects in a GCSE Science and/or Additional Science course (see separate entry for GCSE Science).

GCSE Biology takes the biology from GCSE Science and the biology from GCSE Additional Science, and adds a bit more, to form a qualification which is wholly biology. Students in state-maintained schools must study the complete programme of study, so are required to follow courses in all three separate sciences if they take this pathway.

The principal advantage of taking the single sciences separately lies in keeping a wider range of scientific career routes open.

Main elements of the course

The outline below is based on what the majority of exam board syllabuses include. For an exact definition of the syllabus you will be studying, you should consult your school or the exam board itself.

The main topics in the GCSE Biology course are:

» digestion
» ecology

» ecosystems
» gene technology
» microbes and food
» photosynthesis
» respiration and breathing.

In studying Biology, you will learn about how new knowledge in areas such as genetics, molecular biology, biodiversity and ecology affects human society and the environment all over the planet. You can expect to acquire an understanding of scientific ideas, how they develop, the factors which may affect their development and their power and limitations. You will plan and carry out a range of investigations, considering and evaluating data you have collected yourself and data obtained from other sources. You will learn to evaluate the benefits and drawbacks of scientific and technological developments, including those related to the environment, personal health and quality of life, and consider the ethical issues involved. You will also learn how to select, organise and present information clearly and logically, using appropriate scientific terms and conventions. The use of ICT will play a significant part in much of the teaching and learning.

Human Biology
Some schools and colleges offer Human Biology GCSE as an alternative to Biology. In just the same way as Biology, GCSE in Human Biology is one of the Key Stage 4 GCSE Science subjects that meet the Key Stage 4 Science programme of study.

Human biology is the study of:

» birth and breast feeding
» development and ageing
» disease
» drugs
» genetics and DNA
» green plants as organisms
» health and fitness
» human impact on the environment
» human reproduction and development
» humans as organisms
» inheritance and evolution
» plant and animal cells
» pollution and recycling
» the cultural evolution of humans
» the nature and origin of humans.

How are Biology and Human Biology taught and assessed?

You will be taught how to:

- recognise, recall and show understanding of specific scientific facts, terminology, principles, concepts and practical techniques
- demonstrate understanding of the power and limitations of scientific ideas and factors affecting how these ideas develop
- draw on existing knowledge to show understanding of the benefits and drawbacks of applications of science.

You will also learn how to apply that knowledge and understanding, through analysing and evaluating information and data. You can also expect to learn and apply investigative methods, including skilled practical techniques.

The style and weightings of assessment vary according to the syllabus, but each scheme of assessment has to include a final exam. This written exam accounts for at least 70% of the marks in linear courses and 50% of the marks in modular schemes. Internal assessment accounts for between 20% and 30% of the marks awarded.

The subject at A level

A level Biology covers areas like:

- biological foundations
- human health and disease
- key biological concepts
- transport and exchange in mammals and plants.

Students normally need at least a grade C in GCSE Biology or Science to take up A level Biology, as much of the syllabus requires some prior knowledge. Ability in Mathematics and Chemistry is also useful: students have to collect and input data, as well as understand the chemical processes that take place in the living world.

The subject is also available at AEA level.

Biology and choosing a career pathway

Taking one or more of the separate sciences as a GCSE is the best way of preparing for an A level in the same subject. If you are thinking of a career that is directly related to biology, it is best if you can offer some strength in Mathematics and/or the physical sciences (Physics and Chemistry). With A levels or an equivalent qualification (such as the

BTEC Diploma) you could look at work in healthcare (including nursing), laboratory work, or work in a dental surgery. Fields of graduate employment directly related to Biology include animal care, biotechnology, cytogenetics, medical sales, pharmacology, scientific laboratory work and veterinary science.

Further information

ARKive: www.arkive.org
BBC Science and Nature: www.bbc.co.uk/sn/
Biotopics: www.biotopics.co.uk; www.bbc.co.uk/cbbc/art/
BrainPOP: www.brainpop.com
Digital Brain: ww.digitalbrain.com
Living Library: www.livinglibrary.co.uk
Making Sense of Health: www.makingsenseofhealth.org.uk
S-Cool: www.s-cool.co.uk
Science and Plants for Schools: www-saps.plantsci.cam.ac.uk

Business Studies

Courses in Business Studies and related areas (see variations below) offer students the chance to develop knowledge and understanding of the business world. Learning about how business works also makes young people more aware of their active roles as consumers, workers, citizens and, potentially, as business owners.

GCSE Business Studies

GCSE Business Studies enables candidates to develop an understanding of:

- the relationship between business activity and the changing environment within which it takes place
- the contribution that organisations make to wealth creation and the success of the society in which they operate
- the structure, organisation and control of the main forms of business
- the nature and role of enterprise and business management
- national and international competition
- e-commerce.

It also helps develop communication, planning and evaluation skills and gives young people the knowledge and understanding to use these skills appropriately in the private, public or voluntary sector.

Main elements of the course

The outline below is based on what the majority of exam board syllabuses include. For an exact definition of the syllabus you will be studying, you should consult your school or the exam board itself.

Students are introduced to a balanced range of topics, such as the external environment of a business; business aims, structure, organisation and control; business behaviour; people in a business or organisational environment; aiding and controlling business activity; business communication; finance; marketing; production.

Other GCSE courses offered in this subject area

- Business and Communication Systems
- Business Studies and Economics
- Economics
- Statistics.

Short course

There is also a short course GCSE available in this subject. The main difference is that the course takes half the time allocated to a full GCSE.

See also the introduction to short courses on page 18.

GCSE Applied Business (Double Award)

GCSE Applied Business, like Business Studies, includes the study of the business sector – people, finances, marketing strategy and product planning – and enables students to develop knowledge and understanding of business through the investigation of a range of business organisations. The difference lies mainly in the approach to teaching and learning: Applied Business offers a more practical approach. The course comprises the following three units:

- Unit 1 – Investigating business (internally assessed)
- Unit 2 – People in business (internally assessed)
- Unit 3 – Business finance (externally assessed).

This qualification is a double award, so it is the same value as two GCSEs.

How is Business Studies taught and assessed?

Assessment consists of *either* 100% examination *or* 75% examination with 25% coursework. Where coursework is included, it is likely to consist of two pieces of project work, for example one on marketing and one on recruitment. Candidates are required to demonstrate their ability to apply their knowledge and understanding of the subject content using appropriate terms, concepts and theories to address given problems and issues; to select, organise, interpret and use information from various sources to analyse problems and issues; and to evaluate evidence, make reasoned judgements and present conclusions accurately, within the given case study.

For the Applied Business GCSE, assessment is composed of two-thirds coursework and one-third examination.

Business Studies at A level

Business Studies A levels are available in Business Studies and Applied Business Studies. The main elements of the course include:

- analysis and decision making
- business planning
- business structures, objectives and external influences
- corporate strategy
- financial management
- marketing and production.

The Applied Business Studies course goes into greater detail on some of the business functions/areas of study. Also, students can take options with a more specialised vocational focus.

This subject is also available at AEA level.

Business Studies and choosing a career pathway

The courses provide a good basis for students to build a foundation of knowledge, understanding and skills designed to prepare them for further study or for the world of work. Direct entry is possible at 16 but there are more opportunities available for those who continue with their studies by taking A levels, a BTEC Diploma or a course at the equivalent level. These can lead into jobs in, for example, administration, banking, insurance, management, manufacturing or retail. At graduate level, there is a huge range of opportunities, including accountancy, advertising, banking, distribution/logistics, human resources work, management, marketing, public relations, retail and sales.

Further information

BBC Business: www.bbc.co.uk/business/
Bank of England www.bankofengland.co.uk
Investing for Kids: library.thinkquest.org/3096/
The Times 100: www.thetimes100.co.uk
Young Enterprise: www.young-enterprise.org.uk/pub/
How to Get Ahead In ... Business and Finance, Raintree

Chemistry

Chemistry is the study of:

- » acids and bases
- » atomic structure
- » bonding
- » chemical reactions
- » earth materials
- » metals
- » organic chemicals
- » the periodic table
- » rates of reaction.

GCSE Chemistry

GCSE Chemistry is one of three separate science awards (the others are Biology and Physics) that together cover the requirements of the Key Stage 4 programme of study. You can also combine the study of these three subjects in a GCSE Science and/or Additional Science course (see separate entry for GCSE Science).

GCSE Chemistry takes the chemistry from GCSE Science and the chemistry from GCSE Additional Science, and adds a bit more, to form a qualification which is wholly chemistry. Students in state-maintained schools must study the complete programme of study, so are required to follow courses in all three separate sciences if they take this pathway.

The principal advantage of taking the single sciences separately is that it keeps open a wider range of scientific career routes.

Main elements of the course

The outline below is based on what the majority of exam board syllabuses include. For an exact definition of the syllabus you will be studying, you should consult your school or the exam board itself.

The main topics in the GCSE Chemistry course are:

- acids, alkalis and indicators
- atomic structure and bonding
- chemical calculations
- chemical reactions
- electrolysis
- equilibria
- evolution and maintenance of the atmosphere
- extraction of materials
- geological processes
- industrial processes
- particles
- the periodic table

How is Chemistry taught and assessed?

You will be taught how to:

- recognise, recall and show understanding of specific scientific facts, terminology, principles, concepts and practical techniques
- demonstrate understanding of the power and limitations of scientific ideas and factors that affect how these ideas develop
- draw on existing knowledge to show understanding of the benefits and drawbacks of applications of science.

You will also learn how to apply that knowledge and understanding, through the analysis and evaluation of information and data. You can also expect to learn and apply investigative methods, including skilful practical techniques.

The style and weightings of assessment vary from syllabus to syllabus, but each scheme of assessment has to include a final exam. This written exam accounts for at least 70% of the marks in linear courses and 50% in modular schemes. Internal assessment accounts for between 20% and 30% of the marks awarded.

Chemistry at A level

The main elements of Chemistry at A level include:

- organic and inorganic chemistry; energetics; kinetics; qualitative equilibria

- laboratory chemistry
- periodicity, quantitative equilibria and functional group chemistry
- transition metals, quantitative kinetics and applied organic chemistry.

This subject is also available at AEA level.

Chemistry and choosing a career pathway

Taking one or more of the separate sciences as a GCSE is the best way of preparing for an A level in the same subject. Most jobs using chemistry require high-level qualifications: a degree in Chemistry or a related subject is the most likely entry route for most. Job areas for graduates include analytical chemistry, biochemistry, biomedicine, colour technology, forensic science, industrial research, materials engineering, medical sales, product development, quality assurance, research, scientific journalism, and toxicology.

Further information

BBC Science and Nature: www.bbc.co.uk/sn/
BrainPOP: www.brainpop.com
Digital Brain: www.digitalbrain.com
Doc Brown's Chemistry Clinic: www.wpbschoolhouse.btinternet.co.uk
GCSE Chemistry: www.gcsechemistry.com/ukop1.htm
Mr Guch's Cavalcade o' Chemistry: misterguch.brinkster.net/
chemfiestanew.html
Royal Society of Chemistry: www.rsc.org
S-Cool: www.s-cool.co.uk

Citizenship

Since 2002 all students in England have been required to study Citizenship as a National Curriculum subject. Each GCSE specification must signpost, where appropriate, opportunities for developing citizenship knowledge, skills and understanding.

Courses offer students the opportunity to gain the knowledge, understanding and skills that help enable them to make sense of the society in which they live and to become active members of our democracy.

GCSE Citizenship Studies (short course)
Citizenship is only available as a short course GCSE. A GCSE in Citizenship Studies gives students opportunities to:

- gain knowledge and understanding about becoming informed citizens
- develop skills of enquiry, communication, participation and responsible action
- explore local, national and international issues, problems and events of current interest
- evaluate their participation within school and/or community activities.

As a short course, Citizenship Studies can be joined with another short course GCSE to create one full GCSE.

Main elements of the course
The outline below is based on what the majority of exam board syllabuses include. For an exact definition of the syllabus you will be studying, you should consult your school or the exam board itself.

The GCSE is based on the QCA/DCSF scheme of work for Citizenship at Key Stage 4. The units of study for the scheme of work are:

- business and enterprise
- challenging racism and discrimination
- consumer rights and responsibilities
- crime – young people and car crime
- Europe – who decides?
- global issues, local action
- how and why are laws made?
- how the economy functions
- human rights
- producing the news
- rights and responsibilities in the world of work
- taking part – planning a community event.

How is Citizenship taught and assessed?
In the Citizenship GCSE you can expect to be involved in:

- group and class discussion on events and issues of current interest
- school-based and community-based citizenship activities
- different forms of individual and collective action, including decision making and campaigning
- work with a range of community partners and organisations on issues and problems in communities
- considering the legal, moral, economic, environmental, historical and social aspects of different political problems and issues
- considering a range of contexts (school, neighbourhood, local, regional, national, European, international and global) as relevant to different topics
- using and interpreting different media and ICT
- making links between citizenship and work in other subjects.

Assessment consists of 40% examination and 60% coursework.

Citizenship and choosing a career pathway
Students who are particularly interested in Citizenship studies may wish to look at careers in areas such as the civil service, journalism, the law, local government, the police, or youth or community work.

Further information
21 Citizen: www.21citizen.co.uk/live/citizenship/
Active Citizens in schools: www.continyou.org.uk

Design and Technology

This is a creative and practical subject area. Students learn how products are designed, created and implemented. This includes the creative and artistic design process and design and technology in the industrial context. The subject offers students the opportunity to use tools (including ICT) and materials when designing and making things.

GCSE Design and Technology

Students take part in design and make projects that are linked to their own interests, industrial practice and the community. Projects may involve an enterprise activity, where students identify an opportunity, design to meet a need, manufacture products and evaluate the whole design-and-make process. Students use ICT to help with their work, including CAD/CAM software, control programs and ICT-based sources for research. They consider how technology affects society and their own lives, and learn about the advantages and disadvantages of new technologies.

The main alternatives in GCSE Design and Technology are:

- Electronic Products
- Food Technology
- Graphic Products
- Product Design
- Resistant Materials Technology
- Systems and Control Technology
- Textiles Technology.

Short course in Design and Technology

There is also a short course GCSE available in this subject, while Electronics is also available in its own right as both a short course and a full course GCSE. The main difference is that the short courses take half the time allocated to a full GCSE.

How is Design and Technology taught and assessed?

This subject is taught by a mixture of teacher-led activities and 'hands-on' practical work. Much of the theory is taught through the investigations and challenges. Students are required to prepare and submit a portfolio and/or ICT evidence and a product that demonstrates their knowledge of materials, components, processes and techniques. They also learn how to evaluate their own and others' work and consider the wider effects of design and technology on society. Some group work is usually involved and there may be extensive use of ICT.

Assessment consists of 60% coursework and 40% examination.

Design and Technology (or Product Design) at A level

The main elements of Design and Technology at A level are:

- design and technology capability
- industrial and commercial products and practices
- materials, components and systems
- product development.

Some exam boards offer A levels in different aspects of Design and Technology, such as Fashion and Textiles, Food Technology, Resistant Materials Technology, and Systems Control Technology.

Design and Technology and choosing a career pathway

Design and Technology is a useful subject for those who want to leave school at 16 and take the Apprenticeship route. There are relevant Apprenticeships in construction, manufacturing or engineering. For those with good IT skills, there is the possibility of starting at technician level in computer-aided design or engineering.

At graduate level, related jobs include exhibition/display designer, fashion designer, information scientist, production engineer, production manager, quality assurance officer, technical sales engineer, and textile designer.

Further information

D&T Online: www.dtonline.org
Design Council: www.designcouncil.org.uk
Edu Scan: www.eduscan.info/technology/index.html
How Stuff Works: www.howstuffworks.com

Drama

Drama covers all the different stages involved in putting on a performance, including backstage work such as lighting, costumes and make-up. It involves a lot of practical work, group work and learning how to analyse production techniques.

GCSE Drama

GCSE Drama (or Drama and the Theatre Arts) follows on from the drama work that you will have done at Key Stage 3 (or equivalent). GCSE Drama is an excellent choice for anyone who wants to work in the arts. A GCSE in Drama will give you the opportunity to develop specific creative and imaginative skills as well as more general interpersonal and communication skills. It can help you develop confidence in communicating with other people, leadership skills, the ability to work well in a team, and other skills that are essential in all sorts of work with other people.

Main elements of the course

The outline below is based on what the majority of exam board syllabuses include. For an exact definition of the syllabus you will be studying, you should consult your school or the exam board itself.

The syllabuses offered by the exam boards vary considerably but all include a good mixture of theoretical and practical work. The main elements are:

- ❥ study of drama and theoretical approaches to the medium of drama
- ❥ study of drama texts and the way drama is used both to communicate the playwright's ideas and to develop character portrayal

- candidates look at drama as a medium, its constituent elements and study drama texts
- practical experience of writing, producing or performing in a play.

Students will be able to look at many aspects of devising, producing and performing a play, including set design, costume, make-up, lighting, sound, stage management, as well as acting (including improvisation).

Students can also expect to see professional productions and learn how to develop a critical analysis of their response to such live productions.

How is Drama taught and assessed?

The course is largely practical and you will have the opportunity to create your own work. You will be encouraged to use drama to express your feelings and ideas about a range of issues. You will probably have the choice of being involved in the performance of a play from an existing script or one you can create yourselves.

On the theoretical side, you will study plays written by other people, looking at how playwrights express their ideas about a theme or topic. You will also explore ways in which a play can be made to work effectively on the stage. Much of the work is done in groups.

The exam for GCSE Drama is a practical performance. It is worth 40% of the total marks. You will take part in a play that you have created as a group or rehearsed from a script. You can either be examined on your acting skills in the performance or on your design and technical skills (stage design, costume, masks and make-up, lighting or sound). You will perform the play in front of an audience and the examiner will be present at one of the performances.

For the 60% coursework part of the course you can expect to be assessed on your performance in:

- responding to ideas and issues
- developing and exploring ideas in creating a piece of drama work
- presenting your ideas to an audience
- evaluating your own performance and that of others.

Drama and Theatre Studies at A level

There are courses in Drama and Theatre Studies and in Performance Studies. The syllabuses vary but include the study of texts and preparation for performance, including the full range of drama and theatre activity, including performance, directing, stage design and lighting.

Drama and choosing a career pathway

For a career in performance or on the technical side, it's normally necessary to think in terms of further study. You could go on to take an AS or A level in Drama and Theatre Studies, or an Applied A level in Performing Arts, or a BTEC National Certificate or Diploma in Performing Arts or Performance Design and Technology. Some will then enter theatre work after A levels, aiming to work their way up from backstage or box-office work, or through another junior role in administration.

The orthodox route to becoming an actor or performer is through a degree course or other form of professional training. Other careers, usually at graduate level, include arts administrator, community art worker, drama therapist, journalist, programme researcher, stage manager, television production assistant, theatre director and wardrobe manager.

There are many other jobs, not directly related to theatre, for which it is useful to have had experience of drama, or in which you will need to use some of the skills that can be developed during a GCSE Drama course. These might include jobs in, for example, retail, travel and tourism, sales and marketing, or any area of work that involves meeting and working with people.

Further information

National Association of Youth Theatres: www.nayt.org.uk
National Council for Drama Training: www.ncdt.co.uk

Engineering

Engineering is likely to appeal to you if you are interested in doing and making things, have an inquisitive mind and enjoy solving problems. You'll need to take easily to technical learning and enjoy the idea of working to a design brief and then presenting your solution to an audience or for assessment. Many women make excellent engineers and should not be put off by the wrong-headed idea that engineering is a career sector for boys only.

GCSE Engineering

Engineering is a double award GCSE. This means that the syllabus is equivalent to two standard GCSEs and it takes two years to complete. As a double award, it is worth two GCSE grades. It is a work-related course that allows you to do more practical work alongside the science and technology theory covered in the classroom. It helps you understand how products are made and learn about engineering systems and services.

This is a demanding, technical course and you will need good predicted grades in Mathematics, English and Science if you are to make a success of it.

Main elements of the course

The outline below is based on what the majority of exam board syllabuses include. For an exact definition of the syllabus you will be studying, you should consult your school or the exam board itself.

How is GCSE Engineering taught and assessed?

The course consists of three separate units, equally weighted for assessment purposes:

- application of technology
- design and graphical communication
- ongineored produotc.

For design and graphical communication you'll need to develop a portfolio of work to demonstrate what you know about what you've been taught. You'll learn about the design process, client design briefs, design specifications, solutions, scientific and technological principles, the use of engineering drawings, and the communication of design solutions. You'll be expected to apply the knowledge you've gained to formulate and communicate solutions to technical problems. The portfolio will be internally assessed by your teacher(s).

The engineered products unit is about understanding the process of designing a product and then producing it. It gives you the opportunity to test your planning and design skills. Once you have created a technical design, you'll have to decide how to manufacture it, select the right materials, and ensure you apply quality control measures. Assessment is again via a portfolio and teacher assessment.

In application of technology, you evaluate the problem and assess the evidence provided from measurements that may be mechanical, electrical or statistical. This time your judgements and conclusions are tested through an externally set examination.

Overall, assessment amounts to two-thirds coursework and one-third examination.

Young Apprenticeship in Engineering

Young Apprenticeships are offered in some school/college partnerships. This programme gives young people an opportunity to have some involvement in the workplace. It is aimed at 14-year-olds at Key Stage 4 who are well motivated to learn about and through engineering. The course gives you experience of a real business and technology environment. It offers a broad framework that can include the GCSE in Engineering and this means that your experience of the workplace can enhance and enrich what you learn during lesson time. It allows you to put theory into practice at an engineering training centre or a college of further education and at companies away from school in a real engineering environment.

Applied Engineering at A level

The main elements of Applied Engineering at A level include:

» additional mathematics
» applications of new technology in engineering
» applied mathematics in engineering
» applied mechanics
» applied science in engineering
» applied thermofluids
» computer-aided production engineering
» design development
» electrical and electronic applications
» electrical and electronic principles
» electrical power transmission
» engine technology and transmission diagnostics
» engineering drawing
» engineering in business and the environment
» engineering materials
» engineering processes
» engineering production techniques
» fault diagnosis, maintenance and servicing
» mechanical engineering principles
» mechatronics
» motor vehicle bodywork and repair
» quality assurance and quality control
» robotics.

Engineering and choosing a career pathway

Engineering is a very broad and flexible course, whether you are taking the GCSE or a Youth Apprenticeship (or both). You can use it as a springboard to go on to university or do an Apprenticeship to develop your skills further. There are Apprenticeships in Engineering and Construction available at 16+, but their availability is sometimes limited at local level.

If you wish to work at professional engineering level, you need to plan for continued study to degree level and beyond. The main categories of engineering work are: engineering research and development, engineering design, installation and commissioning engineering, process engineering and customer services, manufacturing and processing, and information technology and management services.

Further information

GCSE in Engineering: www.gcseinengineering.com
Why Study Materials?: www.whystudymaterials.ac.uk
Careers in Engineering, McGraw-Hill
How to Get Ahead In ... Engineering and Design, Raintree

English

English is a compulsory subject at Key Stage 4. This will usually mean taking GCSE English (or English Language). In many schools English and English Literature are taught as a combined course. This can still lead to two distinct qualifications – a GCSE in English and another in English Literature. Entry level English is available for those who may find the GCSE too demanding at this stage.

English is the key subject for learning how to communicate with others in school and in the wider world. Good understanding and use of English is essential for all curriculum subjects. Studying English involves reading various types of texts, writing in different styles, expressing your ideas in both creative and formal ways, listening and discussing.

GCSE English

GCSE English is about acquiring the essential communication skills in speaking, listening, reading and writing. Students learn to express themselves creatively and imaginatively and to communicate with others confidently and effectively. Spelling, grammar and punctuation are integral to studying English.

Main elements of the course

The outline below is based on what the majority of exam board syllabuses include. For an exact definition of the syllabus you will be studying, you should consult your school or the exam board itself.

The main topics include:

- media texts
- original writing

» poetry from different cultures
» reading non-fiction texts
» speaking and listening
» writing to argue/persuade/advise
» writing to explain/inform/describe.

The range of reading varies across England, Wales and Northern Ireland. In all countries the range of reading must include prose, poetry and drama. There will also always be some study of texts from different cultures and traditions. In England, the choice of texts must include:

» a play by Shakespeare
» work from the English literary heritage by at least one major writer with a well-established critical reputation.

In Northern Ireland the range must include:

» work by at least one author published before 1914
» work by at least one major Irish author with a well-established critical reputation whose work was published after 1914.

For Wales the range must include:

» work from the English literary heritage by at least one major writer with a well-established critical reputation
» work by a Welsh author writing in English or that has a Welsh setting or special relevance to Wales.

Variations
Some students might be offered a Certificate in English as an alternative to (or alongside) GCSE English.

How is English taught and assessed?
There will be a considerable amount of teacher-led activity, but you can also expect to participate in a variety of speaking and listening assessments through the course. These contribute to 20% of the final English grade. You will experience a variety of reading that includes drama, poetry, fiction, non-fiction and media texts. There is also a wide range of written work. Coursework assignments can last for several weeks, with part of the work done in class and part at home. Other assessment may include extended individual contributions, group discussion and interaction, and drama-focused activities.

The weighting for assessment in English is up to 40% for the coursework and 60% for the examination component. For Literature, the weighting is 30% coursework and 70% examination.

GCSE English and Functional Skills

In the same way that level 1 Functional Skills in English is part of the Key Stage 3 programme of study for English, the Key Stage 4 programme of study reflects the functional English standards at level 2. The skills specified are based on the functions of speaking, listening, reading and writing. The aim is that each individual should be confident and capable when using these skills and should be able to communicate effectively, adapting to a range of audiences and contexts. This includes being able to explain information clearly and succinctly in speech and writing, expressing a point of view reasonably and persuasively, using ICT to communicate effectively.

In life and work each individual should be able to:

- read and understand information and instructions
- use this understanding to act appropriately
- analyse how ideas and information are presented
- evaluate the usefulness of ideas and information, for example in solving a problem
- make an oral presentation or report
- contribute to discussions and use speech to work collaboratively in teams to agree actions and conclusions.

There should be relevant opportunities and contexts for testing of these functional elements in GCSE English. Schools and colleges are due to introduce the revised GCSE in English, including functional skills, in September 2009.

English/English Language at A level

The main elements include:

- interacting through language
- introduction to language study
- language variation and change
- using language.

The exam boards also offer a combined course in English Language and Literature.

This subject is also available at AEA level.

English and choosing a career pathway

As with the other core subjects (Mathematics and ICT), the relevance of English is far greater in its general application to just about all vocational pathways than it is in any one single pathway. Employers want people who can communicate effectively in both the written and spoken word – and these skills are just as important for the self-employed. In this sense, English is very much a vocational subject. As with the other core subjects, for most of us it supports other job-specific skills: for example, the engineer or architect who wants to progress will need to show good facility in English and communication skills.

For those who do wish to use their English language and communication skills as a central feature of their working lives, there are jobs in, for example, administration, customer service, information science, journalism, marketing and sales, and public relations.

Among the graduate-level areas of employment for the English specialist are: advertising, journalism, marketing, public relations, publishing, teaching (including teaching English as a foreign or second language), and television and film work.

Further information
BBC Skillswise: www.bbc.co.uk/skillswise/
GCSE Guide: www.gcseguide.co.uk
Online English Grammar: www.edufind.com/english/grammar/toc.cfm

English Literature

Literature reflects the experience of people from different countries and different periods of history and contributes to our sense of cultural identity. The study of English literature involves reading stories, poetry and drama, as well as non-fiction and media texts.

GCSE English Literature

GCSE English Literature involves analysing texts, such as novels, poetry and plays, and understanding how writers use language to achieve different effects. Students also have the opportunity to learn about historical and social influences on writing.

Main elements of the course

The outline below is based on what the majority of exam board syllabuses include. For an exact definition of the syllabus you will be studying, you should consult your school or the exam board itself.

GCSE English Literature requires study of a number of different texts, including prose, poetry and drama, both pre- and post-1914.

How is English Literature taught and assessed?

There is a lot of independent reading involved in the study of literature. Classwork involves studying parts of the set texts in detail, but supporting reading will be necessary outside the classroom. English Literature is a demanding subject in terms of both the amount of reading and the number of essays you'll need to write. Students are sometimes encouraged to enact a section of the play they are studying. Group visits to a theatre are sometimes arranged, while you would also be encouraged to make your own individual visits where this is possible and appropriate. It is, of course, particularly beneficial to be able to see a professional production of any play you are actually studying.

The weighting for assessment in English Literature is 30% for the coursework and 70% for the examination.

English Literature at A level

English Literature at A level involves the study of set texts, from drama, poetry and fiction. A Shakespeare play is often one of the set texts.

The choice of poetry may include some of Chaucer's *Canterbury Tales* and/or Shakespeare's sonnets. Other poets studied may include, for example, William Blake, Robert Browning, T. S. Eliot, Seamus Heaney, John Keats, John Milton, Sylvia Plath, Percy Bysshe Shelley, Alfred Lord Tennyson, William Wordsworth.

Pre-twentieth-century writers of fiction may include, for example, Jane Austen, Charlotte Brontë, Emily Brontë, Joseph Conrad, Daniel Defoe, Charles Dickens, Henry Fielding, Elizabeth Gaskell, Thomas Hardy, Henry James, Robert Louis Stevenson, Anthony Trollope, H. G. Wells.

The exam boards also offer a combined course in English Language and Literature.

English Literature and choosing a career pathway

For most students this subject is best regarded as an interesting subject in its own right, rather than one that will link directly with a particular career. However, as with English Language, it is an excellent subject for sharpening one of our most important everyday tools – communication through language. The analytical and critical skills that it helps develop are also advantageous in many jobs.

For those who develop a particular affinity for the study of literature, some jobs do have a clearer relation to this field of study. These include library assistant, marketing, tour guide, and many other jobs that require good communication skills.

At graduate level, jobs for the lover of English literature include advertising, arts administration, journalism, marketing, public relations, publishing, and television and film work.

Further information

National Council for the Training of Journalists: www.nctj.com
SparkNotes: www.sparknotes.com/home/english/

Geography

Geography is about the changing world in which we live, both the physical and the human environment.

GCSE Geography

Geography consists of physical and human geography. Students learn about the environment in which we live and the way that humans interact with and manage that environment.

Main elements of the course

The outline below is based on what the majority of exam board syllabuses include. For an exact definition of the syllabus you will be studying, you should consult your school or the exam board itself.

There are three main areas of study – physical, environmental and human geography. Physical geography involves studying natural features such as weather and climate, rivers and coastal landscapes. Human geography covers population and economic and industrial activity, including agriculture, tourism and manufacturing industry. Environmental geography looks at how the natural environment shapes our lives and examines how human action impacts on the environment, including the use of energy, the management of ecosystems, and the management of change and development. It involves using maps, statistics and photographs, and taking part in field trips.

Short course

The short course GCSE requires half of the study of the full course and can be delivered in half the time allocated to the full GCSE, over two years or in one year with the same timetable commitment as a full GCSE. The content is a subset of the content of the full course, with syllabuses maintaining a balanced approach to the subject.

How is Geography taught and assessed?

Much of the work is teacher-led and there is also an element of learning from textbooks and other materials. However, the subject also involves more practical work – for example, with maps, statistical data, weather reports and case-study material. You will carry out surveys, create questionnaires and watch film or video. The analysis of data is an important aspect of Geography at all levels.

The coursework component accounts for 25% of the final marks. The coursework will usually be based on a single fieldwork-based investigation. The remaining 75% is allocated to examination work.

Geography at A level

The main elements of A level Geography are:

» challenge and change in the natural environment
» core concepts in human geography
» core concepts in physical geography.

This subject is also available at AEA level.

Geography and choosing a career pathway

Relatively few students make active use of geography in their careers. However, the subject encourages the development of a wide range of skills – in research, numeracy and spatial awareness, and in critical and analytical thinking. All of these can be of great value to young people starting on a career, regardless of their age at the point of entry.

Where jobs are more closely related to geography itself, it is normally necessary to study the subject (or a related one) to degree level first. Examples of jobs that do use the skills and knowledge of the geographer include: cartographer, distribution/logistics manager, ecologist, environment consultant, geologist, mining engineer, surveyor, town planner, and transportation planner.

Further information

Association for Geographic Information: www.agi.org.uk
BBC Science and Nature: Earth: www.bbc.co.uk/science/space/solarsystem/earth/

Internet Geography: www.geography.learnontheinternet.co.uk
National Geographic: www.nationalgeographic.com
Royal Geographical Society: www.rgs.org
UK Civil Service Careers: www.civilservice.gov.uk/careers

Health and Social Care

In Health and Social Care you learn about health services, the care industry, the promotion of health and well-being, the nature of personal relationships and the various stages of personal development. You do not need to have studied health or social care before starting the GCSE. It is important that you have a lively and enquiring mind, an interest in the subject area and an ability to communicate your ideas effectively.

GCSE Health and Social Care

This GCSE is a double award qualification, so it is equal to two GCSEs and is twice the size of most GCSEs. It is made up of three units:

» **Health, Social Care and Early Years Provision**
  This involves the study of the three areas of the care industry: healthcare; social care; and early years care. You learn about what each of the services does, the range of jobs involved and how people work together to provide care for different people. You will also find out about the different jobs in the care industry.
» **Promoting Health and Well-being**
  In this unit you will learn about health and well-being, how to encourage and promote good health, deal with emergencies and develop a health plan. You will learn about the role of a balanced diet and of exercise and the effects of working life on health. You also learn how to recognise poor health and poor well-being and how steps can be taken to put things right.
» **Understanding Personal Development and Relationships**
  This includes the study of how people grow and age, both physically and mentally. You find out about the different stages of development and the factors that affect growth and development. You will also look

at the different relationships that people have and the effects of different family circumstances and events.

How is Health and Social Care taught and assessed?
This is an Applied GCSE and its teaching is therefore closely related to the health and care work sector. The subject is taught by a mixture of teacher-led activities and independent coursework, research and reading. Much of the learning is practical. There are likely to be visiting speakers who will talk about their work and/or current issues in the health and social care sector. There may also be group visits arranged to different health and social care settings.

Assessment is weighted in terms of two-thirds coursework and one-third examination.

Applied Health and Social Care A level
The Applied A level course usually includes a mixture of compulsory units and some optional ones, from a range of choices. The core modules include areas such as:

- communication in health and social care
- equal opportunities and clients' rights
- factors affecting human growth and development
- physical aspects of health
- research perspectives in health and social care
- social care and early years services.

Other units fall into three broad categories:

- biological, psychological and medical factors relating to health and social care
- health and social care relating to people in their early years
- healthcare provision and policy.

Health and Social Care and choosing a career pathway
Many students who invest the additional time in taking this sort of applied course will already be actively considering taking up a career in the broad occupational area. Specific jobs include: dental hygienist, health promotion/education specialist, healthcare assistant, mental health nurse, midwife, nurse, nursery nurse, playworker, social worker.

For higher-level occupations in health and social care, you will certainly need to continue your studies to A level (or equivalent) and beyond. If you wish to become a doctor, for example, the preferred route is to take three sciences at A level (or two science A levels plus A level Mathematics). Increasingly, senior jobs in other branches of medicine, health and social care also require graduate entry. Examples include health promotion, health service management, lifestyle coaching and consultancy, medical sales, nursing, nutrition and physiotherapy.

The Diploma in Social Work (DipSW) is currently the professional qualification for all social workers and education welfare officers in England.

Further information
Jobs in community care: www.communitycare.co.uk
NHS Careers: www.nhscareers.nhs.uk
Careers in Health and Social Care, McGraw-Hill
How to Get Ahead in ... Healthcare, Raintree
Working in Community Healthcare, VT Lifeskills
Working in Hospitals, VT Lifeskills
Alexander, Laurel *Nursing and Midwifery Uncovered*, Trotman
Caprez, Emma *Real Life Guide to Care*, Trotman

History

The subject develops a knowledge and understanding of various aspects of the past at a local, national and international level. However, the study of history is not just learning about the past. Developing our view of the past from the perspective of the present can help us interpret and understand current events.

GCSE History

The study of GCSE History helps you develop knowledge and understanding of various aspects of the past with local, national and international significance. The subject also helps develop many useful skills and qualities, including empathy, the critical evaluation of written information and the ability to weigh up evidence.

There are three main courses:

- Modern World
- Schools History Project
- Social and Economic History.

Detailed elements of course

The **Schools History Project** topics are:

- Medicine through Time (ancient medicine, medieval and Renaissance medicine, modern medicine)
- American West
- Germany 1918–1939.

The **Modern World History** topics include:

- Britain 1905–1951
- Germany 1918–1939
- International Relations 1900–1939
- International Relations 1945–1991
- Northern Ireland 1965–1985
- Russia/USSR 1905–1941
- USA 1919–1941
- Vietnam 1954–1975.

British Social and Economic History topics include:

- agriculture 1700–1900
- Chartism
- industry 1700–1900
- transport 1700–1900.

Short course

There is also a short course GCSE available in this subject. The main difference is that the course takes half the time allocated to a full GCSE.

See also the introduction to short courses on page 18.

How is History taught and assessed?

As well as teacher-led activity and group discussion, students have the opportunity to investigate a range of resources, including books, newspapers, artefacts, historical sites and the internet to explore the past. Students need to be aware that, in choosing this subject, they will be required to take on a considerable amount of reading and writing.

Coursework usually accounts for around 20–25% of the total marks; the rest is by examination.

History at A level

The main syllabus variations relate to the type of history studied (social, political or religious history) and a possible focus on a particular period. Most syllabuses include the study of a particular period of English or British history: the courses tend to cover a period of up to 150 years at a time. Students may also have the opportunity to study a period of history other than British or English history. The same applies in terms of the length of period studied, but in general the periods offered for study for European or world history run from about 1000 to 1900 and nothing more recent than that.

Most courses will cover:

- a range of historical perspectives
- a substantial element of English history
- continuity and change over a particular period
- significant historical events, issues or people
- the diversity of society
- the history of more than one country or state.

Some syllabuses include the opportunity to study certain historical themes, for example:

- civil rights in the USA 1865–1980
- rebellion and disorder in England 1485–1603
- the Catholic Reformation in the sixteenth century
- the decline of Spain 1598–1700
- war and society in Britain 1793–1918.

This subject is also available at AEA level.

History and choosing a career pathway

Relatively few students will go on to make active use of their history studies in their working lives. However, the skills and knowledge gained are very useful in a wide range of occupations, including law, management and administration, sales and marketing.

There are a number of jobs that do draw specifically on the skills and techniques of the historian. These include: archaeologist, archivist, costume designer, genealogist, librarian, media researcher, museum work, and tourist guide.

Further information

BBC History: www.bbc.co.uk/history/
Council for British Archaeology: www.britarch.ac.uk
The History Channel's Study Zone: www.historystudystop.co.uk
History Learning Site: www.historylearningsite.co.uk
Museums Association: www.museumsassociation.org
School History: www.schoolhistory.co.uk

Information and Communications Technology (ICT)

ICT is about the purpose and use of communication systems, including how ICT is used to solve problems. You can expect to learn about hardware and software, the effect of new technology on the world and how to present work using ICT.

ICT is a compulsory National Curriculum subject. For most students this will mean taking a GCSE, short course GCSE or Applied GCSE in ICT, a qualification from the DiDA suite of awards (see below), or perhaps entry level ICT.

GCSE ICT

Computers and information technology have clearly come to play a significant part in all our everyday lives. Even if we choose to be more or less passive recipients of the technology, it is all around us, every day of our lives. As a subject, ICT involves the study of how information and communications systems can be used and how they can solve problems. Students have the opportunity to learn about hardware and software, the effect of new technology on the world and how to present their work using ICT.

Main elements of the course

The outline below is based on what the majority of exam board syllabuses include. For an exact definition of the syllabus you will be studying, you should consult your school or the exam board itself.

Topics in GCSE ICT include:

- data communications
- databases

- hardware
- ICT systems
- implications of ICT
- measurement and control
- modelling
- software
- the legal framework.

Applied ICT

Applied ICT is a vocational course that should appeal to you if you like using computers and want to know more about ICT systems, how organisations use ICT, ICT tools, spreadsheets, word processing, presentation techniques and multimedia software.

Short course

There is also a short course GCSE available in this subject. The main difference is that the course takes half the time allocated to a full GCSE.

See also the introduction to short courses on page 18.

DiDA (Diploma in Digital Applications)

DiDA is actually a suite of three qualifications: the Award (AiDA), the Certificate (CiDA) and the Diploma (DiDA). This enables students who opt for this type of ICT qualification to progress through the suite, if they wish and their circumstances permit. The Award is equivalent to one GCSE, the Certificate to two GCSEs and the Diploma to four GCSEs.

These are entirely paperless qualifications that have been designed to equip students with practical and transferable ICT skills. They are intended to enable students to apply their knowledge and skills to real situations. Students present the evidence of their work in an e-portfolio which is assessed and moderated on-screen.

Current DiDA topics include:

- graphics
- ICT in enterprise
- multimedia
- using ICT.

There are plans to offer three new units:

- digital film making
- digital game making
- digital publishing and broadcasting.

How is ICT taught and assessed?

ICT involves studying what information and communication systems can be used for and how they can solve problems. You learn about hardware and software, the effect of new technology on the world and how to present work using ICT.

In ICT, you will learn to:

» use technology well to organise yourself, your work and your learning
» apply ICT to real-world situations when solving problems and carrying out a range of tasks and enquiries
» use your initiative to find out about and exploit more advanced or new ICT tools and information sources
» evaluate your experiences of using ICT
» use ICT in other subjects and areas of learning.

In GCSE ICT assessment is 40–60% coursework plus a written examination for the rest of the marks allocation. For Applied ICT it is two-thirds coursework and one-third written test.

GCSE ICT and Functional Skills

In the same way that level 1 Functional Skills in ICT is an implicit part of the Key Stage 3 programme of study for ICT, the Key Stage 4 programme of study reflects the functional ICT skills at level 2. The aim is that each individual should be confident and capable when using ICT systems and tools to meet a variety of needs in a range of contexts. For example, they will use ICT to find, select and bring together relevant information and use ICT to develop, interpret and exchange information, for a purpose.

In life and work each individual will be able to apply ICT safely to enhance their learning and the quality of their work. There should be relevant opportunities and contexts for testing these functional elements in GCSE ICT.

Schools and colleges are due to introduce the revised GCSE in 2009.

Applied ICT at A level

The main elements of an ICT A level are:

» information systems and communications
» structured practical ICT tasks
» practical applications of ICT using standard/generic applications software

» communications technology and its application
» ICT project
» ICT systems and systems management.

ICT and choosing a career pathway

Whether or not you choose to be an ICT specialist, in most jobs it will be an advantage to have had a good grounding in ICT and to have developed some knowledge of how computers and information technology can be put to best advantage. A good grasp of this field will open up opportunities whether you opt to leave school at 16 or carry on with further studies. The vast majority of organisations rely on IT support in some shape or form.

The higher-level specialist jobs may require degree qualifications, although there are also prestigious non-graduate qualifications that are valued in the industry. Examples of graduate or graduate-level jobs for the IT specialist include: applications developer, artificial intelligence researcher, computer games designer, computer service technician, database administrator, internet/web professional, IT consultant, IT sales professional, multimedia designer, penetration testing consultant, robotics developer, software developer/engineer/programmer, systems analyst/designer/developer, technical support person.

Further information

BBC Webwise: www.bbc.co.uk/webwise/
British Computer Society: www.bcs.org
Computer Information Center: www.compinfo-center.com
ICT Teacher: www.ict-teacher.com/index.html
Jegsworks: www.jegsworks.com
What Is: whatis.techtarget.com
Careers in IT, McGraw-Hill
How to Get Ahead In ... IT and Admin, Raintree
Hobbs, Mike *E-Commerce Uncovered*, Trotman

Leisure and Tourism

The study of Leisure and Tourism relates to a very large and varied work sector. At Key Stage 4, the emphasis is principally on leisure, tourism and travel, but there are links to other areas, such as hospitality and sport.

GCSE Leisure and Tourism

This is a double award GCSE that covers different areas of the leisure, tourism and travel industries, such as holiday resorts, theme parks, travel agencies and air transport. Students will have the opportunity to find out about customer service, marketing and tackling real workplace situations.

Main elements of the course

There are three compulsory units that act as a framework for the course:

» investigating leisure and tourism
» marketing in leisure and tourism
» customer service in leisure and tourism.

For an exact definition of the syllabus you will be studying, you should consult your school or the exam board itself.

How is Leisure and Tourism taught and assessed?

There will be a mixture of teacher-led activity, other classroom work, much research and other, more practical work. There will almost certainly be visits to different locations and organisations that are relevant to the study of this sector.

Assessment is by a combination of externally set and marked written exams and internally assessed portfolios of evidence. The weighting of assessment is two-thirds by coursework and one-third by examination.

Applied Leisure and Recreation A level
The main elements of an Applied Leisure and Recreation A level are:

- business systems in the leisure and recreation industry
- children's play
- countryside recreation
- customer service in leisure and recreation
- financial planning in leisure and recreation
- health and fitness
- human resources in leisure and recreation
- investigating anatomy and physiology
- investigating leisure and recreation
- marketing leisure and recreation
- outdoor activities
- providing coaching sessions
- safe working practices in the leisure and recreation industry
- sponsorship in sport
- sports officiating
- sports tourism
- the sports industry.

Leisure and Tourism and choosing a career pathway
Many students who do invest the additional time in taking this sort of applied course will already be actively considering taking up a career in the broad occupational area. Trainee positions are quite commonly available for those with A levels, for example with travel agencies and companies. Other specific jobs include: air cabin crew, customer services, holiday representative, hotel receptionist/front desk staff, and passenger check-in operator. Graduate jobs include holiday representative, tourism officer, tourist information centre manager, tour manager, and travel agency manager.

Further information
Careers in Leisure and Learning: www.skillsactive.com/careers
Institute of Travel & Tourism: www.itt.co.uk
Travel Industry Jobs: www.travelindustryjobs.co.uk
How to Get Ahead In ... Leisure and Tourism, Raintree
Evans, Sarah *The Travel Industry Uncovered*, Trotman

Manufacturing

The manufacturing sector is made up many different industries and includes, for example, the manufacture of food, drink, textiles, print, biological and chemical goods.

GCSE Manufacturing

A GCSE in Manufacturing is likely to appeal to students who want a broad background in manufacturing and who might wish to progress to further/higher education or employment in the sector. You will also gain an understanding of the contribution that manufacturing makes to society and the economy. You will need a good standard of numeracy and literacy, as well as an interest in designing and making products.

GCSE Manufacturing is a double award GCSE that looks at how products are designed and made, and the importance of materials. Students will have the opportunity to learn how to develop a design specification, draw up a final design, and offer a manufacturing solution.

Main elements of the course

The outline below is based on what the majority of exam board syllabuses include. For an exact definition of the syllabus you will be studying, you should consult your school or the exam board itself.

The essential elements are:

- production details and constraints
- materials, components and/or ingredients and their constraints
- new technology used in and by the manufacturing industries
- impact of modern technologies

- investigating manufactured products
- a range of manufacturing industries.

Students will also be required to design a product and manufacture a product.

How is Manufacturing taught and assessed?

Teaching consists of teacher-led and other traditional classroom activity, along with plenty of more practical work. You will learn how to plan and carry out investigations and tasks, using a range of tools, equipment, materials, components and processes. You will be taught how to analyse issues and problems relevant to manufacturing processes and procedures. You will gather, record and analyse relevant information, data and other forms of evidence. You will learn how to evaluate evidence, make reasoned judgements, and present conclusions accurately and appropriately.

Assessment is by a mixture of written exam and a portfolio of evidence. The weighting of assessment is two-thirds coursework and one-third examination.

Manufacturing and choosing a career pathway

Many students who do invest the additional time in taking this sort of applied course will already be actively considering taking up a career in the broad occupational area. Opportunities in manufacturing and engineering fall into the following broad categories:

- engineering research and development
- engineering design
- installation and commissioning engineering
- process engineering, control and maintenance
- commercial engineering and customer services
- manufacturing and processing
- information technology and management services.

Specific jobs include: electronics assembler, engineering operative, materials technician, product designer, production manager, and quality control inspector.

Further information

Institute of Operations Management: www.iomnet.org.uk
SEMTA: www.semta.org.uk

Mathematics

Mathematics is a compulsory National Curriculum subject at Key Stage 4. This normally means taking a GCSE in Mathematics, but entry level Mathematics is also available for those who might find the GCSE too difficult at this stage. Mathematics involves numbers, algebra, shapes, measurements and learning how to handle information. You also learn how to use your knowledge to solve real-life problems.

GCSE Mathematics
Since Mathematics is a compulsory subject, it is certainly in your best interests to take a GCSE if you are capable of doing so. Mathematics remains a subject with universal value – and is a specific requirement for a vast number of options in both employment and further/higher education.

Main elements of the course
The outline below is based on what the majority of exam board syllabuses include. For an exact definition of the syllabus you will be studying, you should consult your school or the exam board itself.

The topics that are common to GCSE Mathematics, at whatever tier it is studied, include:

» geometry and measures
» number and algebra
» statistics.

The depth and degree of complexity to which each of these topics are studied varies according to the tier for which you are entered: see the paragraph below on tiering.

How is Mathematics taught and assessed?

In Mathematics you can expect to:

- use a range of mathematical methods and techniques
- work on sequences of tasks that involve using the same mathematics in increasingly difficult or unfamiliar contexts, or increasingly demanding mathematics in similar contexts
- work on 'open' and 'closed' tasks in a variety of real and abstract contexts
- work on problems that arise in other subjects and in contexts beyond the school
- work on tasks that bring together different concepts, processes and mathematical content
- become familiar with a range of resources, including ICT.

There are two different, but overlapping, tiers of entry. This allows all candidates, whatever their level of ability, every opportunity to demonstrate what they know, understand and can do. The target levels for each of tier are as follows:

	Tier	GCSE grades targeted
1	Foundation	C – D – E – F – G
2	Higher	A* – A – B – C – D

For candidates sitting GCSE Mathematics up to and including November 2008, assessment in GCSE Mathematics is 20% through coursework and 80% through examination. However, from 2009 onwards GCSE Mathematics will no longer include coursework. All marks will therefore be awarded on the basis of the written examination(s).

GCSE Mathematics and Functional Skills

In the same way that level 1 Functional Skills in Mathematics are an implicit part of the Key Stage 3 programme of study for Mathematics, the Key Stage 4 programme of study reflects the functional Mathematics standards at level 2. The aim is that each individual should have sufficient understanding of a range of mathematical concepts and should know how and when to use them. For example, they should have the confidence and capability to use mathematics to solve problems and to use a range of tools, including ICT as appropriate.

In life and work, each individual should be able to:

- develop the analytical and reasoning skills to draw conclusions
- justify how these conclusions are reached

» identify errors or inconsistencies
» validate and interpret results
» judge the limits of the validity of these results
» use these results effectively and efficiently.

There should be relevant opportunities and contexts for testing of these functional elements in GCSE Mathematics. Schools and colleges are due to introduce the revised GCSE in Mathematics, including functional skills, in September 2010.

Mathematics at A level

A level Mathematics is in effect divided between Pure Mathematics (theoretical mathematics) and Applied Mathematics (the application of the subject to different context and uses). The exam boards tend to give schools and colleges some choice about the options students choose in the different mathematical areas. The main areas of study are:

» discrete mathematics
» mechanics
» pure mathematics
» statistics and probability.

This subject is also available at AEA level.

Mathematics and choosing a career pathway

Although you would not become a professional mathematician on leaving school with GCSEs or even A levels, there are many employers who look for all-round numeracy and/or a particular strength in mathematics. Banking, building society work, insurance, payroll work and retail are examples of areas in which junior positions are available after A levels, if not before.

Graduate jobs related to Mathematics include: accountancy, actuarial work, banking, economic and statistical work, financial advice and planning, insurance and pensions, management consultancy, quantity surveying, and scientific research and development.

Further information

BBC Skillswise: www.bbc.co.uk/skillswise/
Figure it Out: www.bbc.co.uk/worldservice/sci_tech/features/figure_it_out/
GCSE Guide: www.gcseguide.co.uk/
Institute of Mathematics and its Applications: www.ima.org.uk
Key Stage 4 Mathematics: www.digitalbrain.com
Mathematics Careers: www.mathematicscareers.org.uk
Royal Statistical Society: www.rss.org.uk

Modern Foreign Languages

Although foreign languages are no longer compulsory at Key Stage 4, the government takes the view that learning languages is highly desirable for all young people. It views languages as being crucially important in the knowledge society of the twenty-first century and it is committed to improving the teaching and learning of languages in schools. It will introduce an entitlement to languages for all pupils in Key Stage 2 (by 2009/2010). Despite the removal of Modern Foreign Languages from the statutory Key Stage 4 curriculum, it is hoped that there will, over time, be an increase in the number of people studying languages beyond school.

GCSEs in Modern Foreign Languages

If you have shown evidence of some ability in language learning, you should certainly give serious consideration to carrying on with – or even, more rarely, starting – a new language for GCSE study. A GCSE in a modern foreign language is highly regarded by university admissions tutors, while employers also value the inclusion of linguistic ability in the wider range of employability skills. Students who have shown particular talents for language learning should consider the option of taking two foreign languages, where the school's arrangements allow: this may put them at an advantage should they later decide to apply for a degree course in languages.

The modern languages most commonly offered at GCSE by schools and colleges are French, German, Spanish and Italian. Gujarati, Polish, Panjabi, Russian and Urdu are all increasing in importance, while other subjects may be available in some schools. And Welsh is an important element of the curriculum in Wales for those young people for whom Welsh is not their native tongue.

Main elements of the course

The outline below is based on what the majority of exam board syllabuses include. For an exact definition of the syllabus you will be studying, you should consult your school or the exam board itself.

Most language courses build on the work covered at Key Stage 3. The emphasis is on the four languages skills of:

» listening
» reading
» speaking
» writing.

Short course

Short course GCSEs are available in French, German, Spanish and Urdu. The main difference is that the course takes half the time allocated to a full GCSE.

See also the introduction to short courses on page 18.

How are Modern Foreign Languages taught and assessed?

Teaching is by a combination of teacher-led and interactive classroom activity, conversation work, written exercises, listening to the language and reading practice. Great emphasis is placed on communication, especially speaking.

Up to 30% of the assessment is through coursework and tests in listening, reading and speaking. The rest is by examination. Ten per cent of the total marks are allocated to knowledge and accurate application of grammar and structures and the use of dictionaries is no longer permitted.

The examination may be at one of two levels – Foundation and Higher. The decision on each student's entry level is usually made quite late in the course.

Modern Foreign Languages at A level

Most of the modern foreign languages offered at GCSE can also be studied at A level. These include Chinese, Dutch, French, Gujarati, German, Italian, Portuguese, Russian, Spanish and Urdu.

Study of a modern foreign language at A level will include:

» aspects of culture and society
» listening

- reading
- speaking
- writing.

French, German and Spanish are also available at AEA level.

Modern Foreign Languages and choosing a career pathway

Being able to speak another language can be useful in a wide range of careers. For most people fluency in another language is a useful skill to have in a job or career that is not specifically focused on languages, e.g. in engineering, media work, publishing, sales or science. However, some jobs and careers are likely to require more frequent use of linguistic skills. Examples include: courier, holiday representative, hotel receptionist, importer/exporter, interpreter, patent agent, police work, translator, work in the Diplomatic Service, and any job involving work abroad.

Further information

BBC Languages: www.bbc.co.uk/languages/
Centre for Information on Language Teaching and Research: www.cilt. org.uk
Digital Brain French: www.digitalbrain.com
français interactif: www.laits.utexas.edu/fi/index.html
Institute of Linguists: www.iol.org.uk
Institute of Translation and Interpreting: www.iti.org.uk
Learn Spanish – a free online tutorial: www.studyspanish.com/index.htm
Mr Lee's Online Spanish Tutor: www.bloomington.in.us/~rlee/website/tutor1.html

Music

The study of Music offers you the opportunity to develop your performing, composing and listening skills.

GCSE Music

Clearly, an interest in music is a key factor in deciding whether GCSE Music is for you. The wider the range of your musical interests the better. However, you need to be aware that the course will be about much more than listening to, singing or playing music. There is a lot of practical work, but there is also a lot of hard work, some of it of a more theoretical nature. You will need to be well organised and able to use a range of key skills, including problem solving and being able to work well in a team.

The course involves both practical work and theory. Students will have the opportunity to be involved in performing, composing, listening and learning to appreciate music. They will also learn to develop skills as a musician or singer.

Main elements of the course

The outline below is based on what the majority of exam board syllabuses include. For an exact definition of the syllabus you will be studying, you should consult your school or the exam board itself.

You can expect to study:

- ❂ classical orchestral music
- ❂ contemporary music
- ❂ music appreciation

- music for dance
- technical elements of music (devices, instrumentation, melody and harmony, notation, rhythm and metre, and texture)
- world music.

Short course

There is also a short course GCSE available in this subject. The main difference is that the course takes half the time allocated to a full GCSE.

See also the introduction to short courses on page 18.

How is Music taught and assessed?

Teacher-led activity is likely to include the technical study of the way music is made up, the history of music, and the study of world music. There is plenty of practical work too, particularly involving playing, singing and listening.

Assessment may be up to 60% coursework (e.g. solo performing, ensemble performing, musical composition), plus written tests or examination. Part of the written examination might be to listen to a CD and answer questions that draw on a range of topics studied during the course.

Music at A level

An A level in Music offers you the opportunity to develop the performing, composing and listening skills you developed at GCSE level. The course also introduces students to a wide variety of music. The course will include the following elements:

- composing
- history of music
- listening comprehension
- performance
- understanding the mechanics of music.

There is also an A level in Music Technology. There is some overlap with A level Music, but here the emphasis is always on how technology is used in relation to musical traditions or styles. There is also a greater emphasis on analysing modern popular music.

Music and choosing a career pathway

Those who do wish to earn their living through music need to know that many areas of the work are extremely competitive and very high-level skills are therefore necessary. Some performers work semi-professionally, typically working in the evening or at weekends to supplement another source of income.

Examples of jobs and careers in music include: composer, disc jockey, music therapist, musical instrument maker/repairer, musical journalist, musician, private music teacher, promotion assistant or manager, and singer. For many of these jobs a degree is at least helpful, although still not a guarantee of finding a career in a very popular occupational sector.

Further information

BBC Music: www.bbc.co.uk/music/
British Society for Music Therapy: www.bsmt.org
The MusicLand: www.themusicland.co.uk
Music at School: www.musicatschool.co.uk
Working in Music, VT Lifeskills
Britten, Anna *Working in the Music Industry*, Trotman
Davies, Sarah and Laing, David *Guerrilla Guide to the Music Industry*, Trotman
Harrison, Ann *Music: The Business*, Virgin Books
Pattenden, Sian *How to Make It in the Music Business*, Trotman
Shillam, Tania *Music Industry Uncovered*, Trotman

Physical Education

PE covers many areas, including health and exercise, sport and recreation. It develops the competence and confidence to take part in different physical activities and involves learning about the value of a healthy, active lifestyle. Students of PE develop a wide range of skills and the ability to use tactics, strategies and ideas to perform successfully.

GCSE Physical Education

Although there is an obvious appeal for students who have already discovered they have outstanding talent in aspects of sport or physical education, the subject is not exclusively for them. It is likely to appeal to anyone with an interest in physical activity and performance. You learn how to exercise safely and effectively to improve health and well-being.

Main elements of the course

The outline below is based on what the majority of exam board syllabuses include. For an exact definition of the syllabus you will be studying, you should consult your school or the exam board itself.

A GCSE in PE involves developing your practical sporting skills in four different activities. You are able to make a guided choice from a wide range of National Curriculum Areas of Activity. These Areas of Activity include:

- adventure activities
- athletics
- dance
- exercise

- games
- gymnastics
- swimming.

The course will also include the study of the following topics:

- anatomy and physiology
- health and fitness
- safety and risk assessment
- sporting culture and history
- training and performance.

Variations
Physical Education: Dance; Physical Education: Games.

Short course
There is also a short course GCSE available in this subject. The main difference is that the course takes half the time allocated to a full GCSE.

See also the introduction to short courses on page 18.

How is PE taught and assessed?
You should expect some formal teaching – for example about tactics, the rules of particular sports, anatomy and physiology – as well as plenty of opportunity for practical work in and around your chosen sporting activities.

You will be assessed during the course and in the final practical assessment on your performance in your selected activities. You will also learn how to assess and analyse the performance of others. Sixty per cent of the marks are awarded for coursework (including the assessment of performance), 40% for the exam.

For the short course, 70% of the marks are awarded for coursework, and 30% via the examination. The written paper may include multiple-choice and short-answer questions.

A level PE
In A level PE you learn about specific physical activities and develop the skills of planning, performing and evaluating these activities. You also gain an insight into the historical and social context of sport, as well as the relationship between psychology and physiology in sport.

The main elements of the course are likely to include:

- the social basis of sport and recreation
- enhancing performance
- principles and methods of exercise and training
- comparative investigation of sport and recreation.

PE and choosing a career pathway

There is more variety in entry level in this occupational sector than with many others. It is possible to get into some sports-related areas without A levels (or equivalent), though they are usually an advantage. Work in leisure clubs and gyms, for example as an assistant, health and fitness instructor or swimming pool attendant may be available at this level.

You usually need a combination of sporting prowess and qualifications to take up a job in coaching and personal training. Having a degree (or equivalent) is becoming increasingly necessary in jobs such as fitness or leisure centre manager, outdoor pursuits manager, physiotherapist, sports administrator, sports development officer, and sports therapist.

Further information

BBC Health: www.bbc.co.uk/health/
BBC Science and Nature – Human Body and Mind: www.bbc.co.uk/science/humanbody/
British Association of Sport and Exercise Sciences: www.bases.org.uk
PE Centre GCSE: www.physicaleducation.co.uk/GCSE/gcse.htm
S-Cool PE GCSE: www.s-cool.co.uk
Sport England: www.sportengland.org
UK Sport: www.uksport.gov.uk
Working in Sport, Trotman
Dixon, Beryl *Sport and Fitness Uncovered*, Trotman

Physics

Physics is the study of how the physical world works. It helps us to:

- learn how scientific work is evaluated, published and verified by the scientific community
- gain an understanding of how physics is used in the modern world
- explore the properties of motion, nuclear physics, energy transfer and electricity
- develop a better awareness of how advances in science and technology affect the world.

GCSE Physics

GCSE Physics is one of three separate science awards (the others are Biology and Chemistry) that together cover the requirements of the Key Stage 4 programme of study. You can also combine the study of these three subjects in a GCSE Science and/or Additional Science course (see separate entry for GCSE Science).

GCSE Physics takes the physics from GCSE Science and the physics from GCSE Additional Science, and adds a bit more, to form a qualification which is wholly physics. Students in state-maintained schools must study the complete programme of study, so are required to follow courses in all three separate sciences if they take this pathway.

The principal advantage of taking the single sciences separately lies in keeping a wider range of scientific career routes open.

Main elements of the course

The outline below is based on what the majority of exam board syllabuses include. For an exact definition of the syllabus you will be studying, you should consult your school or the exam board itself.

The main topics in the GCSE Physics course are:

- electricity and magnetism
- energy resources and transfer
- forces and motion
- radioactivity
- the characteristics of waves
- the earth, solar system, stars and the universe.

How is Physics taught and assessed?

You will be taught how to:

- recognise, recall and show understanding of specific scientific facts, terminology, principles, concepts and practical techniques
- demonstrate understanding of the power and limitations of scientific ideas and factors affecting how these ideas develop
- draw on existing knowledge to show understanding of the benefits and drawbacks of applications of science.

You will also learn how to apply that knowledge and understanding through the analysis and evaluation of information and data. You can also expect to learn and apply investigative methods, including skilful practical techniques.

The style and weightings of assessment vary between different syllabuses, but each scheme of assessment has to include a final exam. This written exam accounts for at least 70% of the marks in linear courses and 50% in modular schemes. Internal assessment accounts for between 20% and 30% of the marks awarded.

Physics at A level

A level Physics is intended to help you to understand how the physical world works and will help you to establish links between theory and experiment. The main elements of the course include:

- electricity and thermal physics
- forces and fields
- materials
- mechanics and radioactivity

- nuclear and particle physics
- patterns and particle accelerators
- wave physics.

This subject is also available at AEA level.

Physics and choosing a career pathway

Taking one or more of the separate sciences as a GCSE is the best way of preparing for an A level in the same subject. For most jobs that make direct use of physics, you need to be thinking in terms of at least a first degree. Some forms of work as a laboratory technician would be a possibility with A levels (or equivalent).

Graduate jobs related to physics include: electronics engineer, geoscientist, materials engineer, medical physicist, meteorologist, research scientist, and scientific laboratory technician.

Further information

BBC Science and Nature: www.bbc.co.uk/sn/
BrainPOP: www.brainpop.com
Digital Brain: www.digitalbrain.com
Fear of Physics: www.fearofphysics.com
Institute of Physics: www.iop.org
Physics and Astronomy online: www.physlink.com

Religious Studies

Religious Studies looks at the purpose of life and the fundamental moral, philosophical and spiritual questions. It includes the study of the various systems of beliefs that have at their centre a belief in the existence of a god or gods.

GCSE Religious Studies

Religious Studies is not only for students who have a religious faith. It explores a range of religious beliefs and experience and looks at the place of religion in the world today.

The course will develop your knowledge and understanding of one or more of the following religions: Buddhism, Christianity, Hinduism, Islam, Judaism and Sikhism. It will also introduce you to important moral, philosophical and spiritual questions, and help give you the skills to deal with them.

Main elements of the course

The outline below is based on what the majority of exam board syllabuses include. For an exact definition of the syllabus you will be studying, you should consult your school or the exam board itself.

The topics studied will include some of the following:

- » death and the afterlife
- » religion and equality, prejudice and discrimination
- » religion and human relationships
- » religion and medical ethics

- religion, peace and justice
- religion, poverty and wealth
- religion, science and the environment
- sanctity of life
- the concepts of good and evil
- the nature of God
- war and peace.

Variations

Religious Studies: Philosophy and Ethics
OCR offers full and short versions of this course, which comprises the study of Christianity and/or one or two other principal religions. The full course is divided into ten topics of study. Candidates study four of topics 1–5 and four of topics 6–10:

1. the nature of God
2. the nature of belief
3. religion and science
4. death and the afterlife
5. good and evil
6. religion and human relationships
7. religion and medical ethics
8. religion and equality
9. religion, poverty and wealth
10. religion, peace and justice.

Short course
There is also a short course GCSE available in this subject. The main difference is that the course takes half the time allocated to a full GCSE and covers only half the subject area (or half the number of topics studied in the full course, as in the OCR course described above).

See also the introduction to short courses on page 18.

How is Religious Studies taught and assessed?
Assessment may be either entirely through examination or by a combination of exam and coursework. In the latter case, this usually means a ratio of something like 20% coursework to 80% exam.

Religious Studies at A level
A level Religious Studies considers the fundamental questions of human existence, examining issues such as the interaction between

religion and science. The main elements of the course are likely to include:

» developments in Christian thought
» other world religions, including Islam, Buddhism and/or Hinduism
» philosophy of religion
» religious ethics
» religious texts, including Jewish scriptures and the New Testament.

This subject is also available at AEA level.

Religious Studies and choosing a career pathway

There are few jobs directly related to Religious Studies below degree level. Becoming a minister of religion or a teacher of religious studies are the most clearly related graduate career options. Other jobs in which you might benefit from a religious studies background include charity worker, counsellor, foreign affairs journalist, police officer, religious worker or leader, social worker, or youth and community worker.

Further information

BBC Religion and Ethics: www.bbc.co.uk/religion/
Church of England: www.cofe.anglican.org
Comparative Religion: www.comparative-religion.com
Council of Christians and Jews: www.ccj.org.uk
Hinduism for Schools: www.hinduism.fsnet.co.uk
Introduction to Sikhism: www.sikhs.org/summary.htm
Islamic Foundation: www.islamic-foundation.org.uk
Judaism 101: www.jewfaq.org/index.htm
National Society for Promoting Religious Education: www.natsoc.org.uk

Science

Science is the field of study that attempts to describe and understand the physical nature of the universe. The government takes the view that everyone needs a basic understanding of science and technology. Science is therefore a compulsory subject at Key Stage 4. However, a traditional approach to science does not suit everyone, so the government has encouraged the development of a range of courses at Key Stage 4.

GCSEs in Science

GCSE qualifications in the sciences are required to meet two quite different needs: first, to prepare all students for their future roles as consumers and citizens in the twenty-first century, in which science is a central part of everyday experience; and second, to prepare future scientists for specialist science studies at A level and beyond.

There have been changes to the statutory programme of study for Key Stage 4 in recent years, with greater emphasis now placed on the nature of science – 'how science works'. The new approach includes an understanding of correlation, the use of evidence and the nature of risk. The vast majority of students will take one or more GCSEs in the subject area. The main options are:

- » GCSE Science, taken on its own
- » GCSE Science and GCSE Additional Science (two separate GCSEs)
- » GCSE Applied Science – a double award which is worth two GCSEs
- » the three Science GCSEs (Biology, Chemistry and Physics) taken separately.

Main elements of the course

The outline below is based on what the majority of exam board syllabuses include in the range of courses. For an exact definition of the syllabus you will be studying, you should consult your school or the exam board itself.

GCSE Science

GCSE Science aims to develop scientific literacy. The two main strands are:

» key scientific explanations which help us to make sense of our lives
» ideas about science which show how science works.

The core topics in GCSE Science are Biology, Chemistry and Physics (see separate entries on these for the sort of topics you can expect to cover).

GCSE Additional Science

GCSE Additional Science builds on GCSE Science by enabling students to acquire the knowledge, understanding and skills needed for future study – to AS and A levels (or equivalent) and beyond – in Engineering, Medicine or other fields of science.

GCSE Applied Science

Applied Science is a double award GCSE which will appeal to you if you want to find out more about how science meets the needs of society. It is intended for those with an interest in the practical application of science; you will learn how science is used in everyday life. Students learn the importance of standard operating procedures and how to apply them in problem solving, and there is a strong focus on work-related learning. You will develop the practical scientific capability needed for jobs in, for example, agriculture, communications, healthcare, manufacturing and technical quality assurance.

GCSEs in Biology, Chemistry and Physics

See the separate descriptions of these subjects under Biology, Chemistry and Physics respectively.

Other variations

» Agricultural Science
» Environmental Science
» Land-based Science
» Rural Science.

Entry level Science

Entry level is for students working below GCSE level. The course consists of a series of short topics with an emphasis on hands-on practical work. Entry level (Science plus) is also available for those who may find a GCSE in Science too demanding at this stage.

How is Science taught and assessed?

Although there is considerable variation between the different syllabuses and the way they are taught, you can expect to learn about the relationships between data, evidence, theories and explanations, and develop your practical and enquiry skills. You will also be helped to develop your ability to communicate your ideas with clarity and precision. All students learn about the applications and implications of science in the modern world and there are opportunities to develop the knowledge, understanding and skills that provide the basis for further studies in science and related areas.

In the Science courses assessment weightings vary. Between 25% and 75% of the marks can be allocated to coursework, the rest by examination. All Science GCSEs are single awards except for Applied Science, which is a double award.

Applied Science A level

The emphasis, as in GCSE Applied Science, is on learning about how science is applied in practical ways, in business, in research or in any other way that is practical or that affects people's lives. The main elements include:

» analysis
» data handling
» energy
» evaluation of the investigation
» health and safety in organisations using science
» health science
» planning and carrying out an investigation
» practical techniques and procedures
» processing and presenting data in an investigation
» science and the community
» study of organisations using science.

Science and choosing a career pathway

You should look at the information given under each individual science (Biology, Chemistry, Physics). Many jobs need science subjects and taking just a single science subject may limit your job or career options, so you do need to research your choices very carefully.

Further information
BBC Science and Nature: www.bbc.co.uk/sn/
BrainPOP: www.brainpop.com
Digital Brain: www.digitalbrain.com
Forensic Science Society: www.forensic-science-society.org.uk
Institute of Biomedical Science: www.ibms.org
Institute of Physics: www.iop.org
NHS Careers: www.nhscareers.nhs.uk
Royal Society of Chemistry: www.rsc.org/chemsoc

Other subjects available at GCSE

Accounting
Arabic
Archaeology
Astronomy
Bengali
Biblical Hebrew
Catering
Chinese
Classical Civilisation
Classical Greek
Dutch
Economics
Electronics
Engineering
Environmental Science
Expressive Arts
General Studies
Gujarati
Health and Social Care
Humanities
Human Physiology and Health
Irish

Japanese
Latin
Law
Leisure and Tourism
Manufacturing
Modern Greek
Modern Hebrew
Panjabi
Performance Arts: Dance
Persian
Media Studies
Polish
Portuguese
Psychology
Russian
Social Science
Statistics
Travel and Tourism
Turkish
Urdu
Welsh

PART THREE: EXAMS AND BEYOND

Making a success of your studies: revision tips

In this section you will:
- *find out how you learn effectively*
- *learn how to prepare effectively for exams*
- *discover how exam boards assess students' work*
- *think about ways of improving your exam technique.*

How do you learn best?

Once you have made the choices about *what* you're going to study at Key Stage 4, it's a good idea to decide *how* you're going to study. There are many different ways of studying and revising and you need to find the approach and techniques that work best for you. You may already have been introduced to some of the theory in 'how to study' sessions at school – or you may have been given a study guide. If so, you'll probably have some idea of what sort of learner you are.

- Visual learners learn best by seeing or visualising things.
- Auditory learners remember what they hear.
- Kinaesthetic learners are hands-on learners who need to feel and touch things.

Whatever your strengths and weaknesses as a learner, you can adopt strategies and techniques that will enable you to play even more to your strengths and to help you overcome your weaker areas.

Your strategy for success

As well as taking into account how your brain works best, there are plenty of other practical things you can do to make your studies as successful as possible. Success in courses like GCSE comes down to four things:

- being organised
- understanding what the exam board wants

» revision
» assessment/exam technique.

Let's look at each in turn.

Get organised!

Here are some tips for organising and getting the greatest benefits from your homework, coursework and any additional study you are doing during Key Stage 4.

When and where?

» Be honest with yourself: don't just opt to study at the times that best suit your social life.
» If you leave homework and other home study until the last minute, the chances are that you'll be too tired or just won't have the time to do the job properly.
» Studying during the day is usually better than studying at night, though it is sometimes a good thing to review key learning points just a little while before you go to bed (they tend to stay with you and be fresh in your mind the next day).
» Try to find a quiet place, free from disturbances or distractions.
» Draw up a regular schedule to help you plan your study or revision.

Smart reading

If you have a lot of reading – and you probably will in at least some of your GCSE subjects – it pays to be efficient in the way you approach it.

» Try to develop a form of speed reading. Instead of reading every word, try 'skimming' the text. This might mean, for example, reading the chapter and sub-headings, plus just the first sentence of each paragraph.
» You can then check your understanding of the text with a more detailed and thorough reading of the same chapter or passage.
» Your quicker reading technique will be particularly useful when it comes to revising, as you won't have time to read everything all over again.

Make note-taking your servant and not your master

» Taking notes in class is very important, and you'll get the best out of them if you can find time to review them later the same day.
» Mark and highlight important information, key ideas, interesting facts and worthwhile quotations while you are reading (but not in a library book!).

- Write important words and phrases on post-its and stick them where you'll see them often.
- Make audio notes by reading your notes onto your mobile phone or a cassette. You can do this with quotations that you want to remember too.
- Try mind mapping – the technique of writing a heading in the middle, circling it, and then drawing out associations from it (for further information on Mind Maps, see www.mind-mapping.co.uk/mind-maps-examples.htm).

Summarising

- Try typing up your summary notes on the important section of a book – or other source material – on your computer. The process of writing up the notes (and thinking about how best to summarise the material) helps you commit them to memory.
- Copy out key points from your notes onto small revision cards. You can even summarise the summary so that you have something really manageable to remember.
- Often the key points are made in the first sentence of each paragraph. Even when this is not the case, you can quickly get into the habit of drawing out the key point from each paragraph or section of a chapter.

Music while you work?

- Listening to music is a great aid to study for some, but it doesn't suit everyone. For some of us, it can be a distraction.
- You may find that it works for you if you select soft, relaxing music – not necessarily your favourite heavy metal tracks.
- Instrumental music tends to work better, as you don't catch yourself listening out for the words. And you may want to turn the volume down lower, so that the music really is just a background to your study.

Get a study buddy

- One of the most effective ways of learning is explaining to others what you have learned.
- It's a two-way process. You will understand and remember more when you listen to someone else give their take on a piece of text you have both been studying.
- A study buddy doesn't have to be one of your best friends. For example, you could share work in a couple of subjects with someone who is stronger than you in one subject, but who has more difficulties than you in another.

- You could also get friends or family to test you on various aspects of your work.

Colour

- You might find the use of colour helpful: not everything has to be written on white paper!
- You could try using different coloured paper for different subjects, at least for taking notes: your teachers may not appreciate colour-coded homework!

Get physical!

- Getting the physical things right for study is really important.
- Make sure you are getting enough sleep and try to come to your study rested and relaxed.
- Take a short break every now and again: it's very difficult to sustain true concentration for more than an hour or so at a time.
- Drink plenty of water, to stay hydrated.

Understanding what the exam boards want

How GCSEs (and other Key Stage 4 qualifications) are assessed varies from subject to subject, but there are many elements that are common to most of them. Some of these are outlined below.

Skills

These days syllabuses are called specifications. You are assessed on the skills you've developed as well as the knowledge you've acquired. All specifications are intended to build on the knowledge, understanding and skills established by the National Curriculum *and* to assist progression to higher qualifications. Both exams and coursework test a number of subject-based skills, such as evaluating, problem-solving and applied engineering skills in Engineering and reading, listening and writing in Modern Foreign Languages.

The government considers that GCSEs should make a strong overall contribution to the way that young people are prepared for – and prepare themselves – to play an active, effective and satisfying role in our society. Its vision is that all people should become:

- creative thinkers
- effective participants
- independent enquirers
- reflective learners

- self managers
- team workers.

This is why so much emphasis is now being placed on functional skills (English, Mathematics and ICT) and on a range of personal, learning and thinking skills. Where possible and appropriate, each GCSE subject makes a contribution to the functional skills and to a range of other skills, such as:

- the ability to communicate well, both individually and in groups
- time management, personal organisation and action planning
- presentational skills
- the ability to reflect and review your own performance and those of other people.

Coursework

As you will have seen from Part Two, most subjects have an element of coursework. The more practical subjects usually contain more coursework and the assessment ratio is weighted more towards some form of 'controlled assessment' than towards exams.

Despite the reservations that are sometimes expressed about coursework (because of the difficulties of supervision and control), it has been widely praised for allowing candidates to demonstrate what they know, understand and can do. It remains an important aspect of the way GCSEs are assessed. It allows a wider range of skills to be assessed than is possible in a written examination. Evidence suggests that coursework assessment increases candidates' motivation.

- If you are a good communicator you'll have the chance to prove it.
- If you are a painstaking perfectionist you'll have the time to research, collect and organise information or data – and earn high marks for your efforts.
- If you are a thinker you'll have time to think.
- If you are a problem solver you'll get the time to find the solution.

Coursework encourages you to work independently and will therefore also help you prepare for higher-level studies, such as AS and A levels. The skills you develop through coursework are also exactly the same sort of work skills that employers value.

Make sure you use the additional opportunity that coursework gives you to demonstrate your skills, knowledge and understanding to your best advantage. It's no good leaving everything to the last minute with coursework, any more than it is with revision for a more formal exam.

You won't get through by rushing to complete an assignment just before the deadline, any more than you will by copying someone else's notes the day before the exam. Unfortunately, many young people end up with a lower grade than their ability deserves because of their failure to complete acceptable coursework. You need to work throughout the two years to do well – and work hard.

Coursework overload is a possible risk with the GCSE and this is a factor you might do well to consider when choosing your range of GCSEs. Once you are on your GCSE programme of studies, your teachers should be working together to ensure that coursework does not become an excessive burden for you. Nobody can tackle a huge number of assignments at the same time and do them all well – and your teachers will want you to do well.

In a well-run school, coursework overload should not happen. But even the best-run systems can break down. So ... if you are given too much coursework at any one time, don't keep your worries to yourself. Tell your teachers about the problem immediately.

No doubt you will find yourself working harder than before, but remember that your teachers are not trying to work you to a standstill. It is in their interests as well as yours that you should do well.

Coursework will normally be marked by your subject teacher in the first instance. A sample of the work marked is then sent to the exam board to be moderated. There is a chance that the work could be marked down by the moderator, so bear in mind that the mark awarded by your teacher is not necessarily the final mark!

Grading and grade boundaries

Grade boundaries are set very carefully by the exam boards. Criteria are set across particular grade boundaries and it is important that these criteria are met each year. Each year, once all the marking is complete, there is a meeting of chief examiners and assessors. This is when the exam board decides the number of marks needed for each grade and ensures that the standard is the same as in previous years. If more students meet the criteria, then more will be awarded the grades. If fewer do, then the opposite will be the case. This system, called 'criteria-referencing', has the advantage of giving a good indication as to whether standards are falling or rising.

As for the grades themselves, much depends on the user. Many employers will stipulate a requirement for a certain number of GCSEs at grades A*–C (or sometimes D). You will normally require at least a grade C in any subject you want to pursue at A level (or equivalent). In some subjects sixth-form and college teachers/tutors will sometimes suggest that only a Grade A or B shows the level of ability needed to cope with higher-level study (although most will be prepared to look at any individual circumstances that may have affected the grade award).

None of this should obscure the fact that a GCSE grade of any sort is an achievement for the individual student. Always listen carefully to the advice of your teachers as to whether the GCSE is the appropriate course for you.

Tiers and grades

Different subjects are organised in slightly different ways. In some subjects, such as Art and Design, History and Music, everybody studying the subject sits exactly the same exam paper.

In other subjects, like English, Mathematics, Science and most foreign languages, there is a choice of different tiers. Each tier has a different target range of grades. The foundation tier assesses grades G to C and the higher tier assesses grades D to A*.

It is for you and your teachers to decide which tier you should enter for those GCSE subjects in which tiering is available. You should always speak to your teachers if you have any concerns about which tier you should be entered for. They will be able to advise you on the choice of tier that is likely to give you the best opportunity to achieve the highest grade of which you are capable – and this is the basic purpose of tiering.

Revision technique

Once the bulk of the formal teaching for your GCSE programme has been completed, your teachers will be encouraging you to start consolidating your learning through revision. There are many ways to revise, and different things work for different people. Review the tips given under 'Get organised!' on page 128. And here are a few additional tips relating specifically to revision. Always work out what works best for you.

- Draw up a revision plan and timetable. Work out when your exams are and how much time you're likely to need to revise thoroughly for each one. Don't leave this too late or too near to the start of your exams. Once you have drawn up the timetable, make sure you stick to it.
- As with coursework, it is always best to find somewhere quiet to work.
- Go to a good bookseller to see a range of revision guides. It could be worth getting one for any subject in which you feel you need particular help.

⊗ Find out where your exams are and when they start, how long they are and what equipment you are allowed to take in (calculators, for example) and what you are not allowed to take in (mobile phones will normally not be allowed!).

⊗ Try to have one weekend day when you don't do revision or think about exams – you should then be able to come back to your studies refreshed.

⊗ People learn – and revise – in different ways. For example, if you think you revise effectively by listening, you could record your revision material and listen to it while lying in bed, while travelling in a car or walking around town.

⊗ Working with someone who is following the same course – not necessarily your best friend – is sometimes a good idea. For example, it can work well if you are studying the same play or novel for English Literature; you may each have different views and approaches that will help the other person see different perspectives and interpretations. But if you choose to work in this way try to make sure it's with someone who won't distract you from the work you're doing.

⊗ Work through some old exam papers – you may be able to get samples from your teacher(s). If possible, it's best to do this under something like exam conditions, in a quiet room and giving yourself the exact amount of time that's meant to be allocated.

Assessment/exam technique

It will always be the case that some people are happier than others in an examination situation. But try to avoid telling yourself you are bad at exams. Coping with exams and performing well in a relatively pressured situation are things that can be learned – and you can get better at them.

⊗ The key factor is being well organised: you will feel more confident about an exam if you have had a revision plan and have put it into practice.

⊗ Before the exams, have a look at the exam board's specification, to see what is required to achieve the different grades. Look at past papers to give you an idea of the types of questions you may be facing.

⊗ In the case of coursework, before you hand in any work, make sure it meets the requirements explained by your teacher.

⊗ Once you are in the exam room, try to stay calm. If you do start feeling anxious, breathe slowly and deeply – it does help.

⊗ Don't worry about how other people are behaving, for example if they seem to be getting straight down to writing an answer. This probably means they have not read the question properly or thought about the best way to answer it.

- There should be time to read the paper, so use that time. Time taken at the beginning to plan your approach will be time well spent.
- Make sure you read all the instructions carefully. If there is a choice of questions, work out carefully which ones you are going to tackle. You need to decide roughly how long you need to allocate to each question or section of the exam.
- Then it may be a good idea to tackle first the questions where you have more knowledge at your fingertips. But keep to your time plan and leave sufficient time to tackle the question(s) you think you will find more difficult.
- Build in time to structure your answer. Jot down as rough work the points that you think the examiner might be looking for in particular – or which you think are critical in answering the question.
- Write clearly and neatly.
- If you finish the exam early, go back and check over your work. Remember to check spelling, grammar and punctuation. You may not feel like doing this, but motivate yourself by telling yourself that it could mean the difference between one grade and the next!

Special arrangements for taking exams

It's possible that there may be some physical reason why you might worry about being at a disadvantage in a formal examination. For example, you may have a particular learning difficulty associated with reading or writing, or English might not be your own first language. In circumstances like these, the awarding bodies aim to give students every opportunity to demonstrate the true levels of knowledge, understanding and skill they have acquired during the course. Sometimes, this might just mean being allowed some extra time to sit the exam. On other occasions, it might mean having an 'amanuensis' – someone appointed to write down a student's answers if, for example, they have a broken arm at the time of the exam.

In most cases, your school will be well informed about any specific difficulty you have and will make sure that the exam boards are also aware of it. You should still check that you will get whatever help you need. Speak to your teachers or to the head of special needs: they should be able to tell you more about any special arrangements offered by the exam board and advise you on how to access them.

After the exam

Once you have completed an exam, it is best to put it behind you and prepare for the next one – or celebrate if it's the last one! Don't be put off by what others say about how well or badly they have handled an exam paper: there is very often little relationship between what is said in these conversations and the eventual results.

When the results come

Normally, you will know that the grade awarded is a very fair indication of your ability and efforts. If you had the ability to do well, but just didn't, work hard enough, you are the one who best knows this.

Just occasionally, though, both you and your teachers may feel that the system has let you down in some way and that something may have gone wrong in the marking process. If this does happen to you, you should take action immediately. You will need to work through your school. They can ask for a 'clerical check', which means your paper is re-marked and the marks added up again. They can also request a complete re-marking of your written papers.

Your school can even request a photocopy of your exam papers from the exam board so that they can check how your papers have been marked. Fees are charged by the exam boards for these services, but any fees are returned if it eventually emerges that the exam board has made a mistake in its marking of your paper(s).

If this process does not result in a revision of your grade and you are still not happy about the outcome, your school can appeal to the exam board, especially if they think that that the correct procedures may not have been followed. If this appeal is unsuccessful, the school can take the appeal to the independent Examinations Appeals Board.

It is worth pointing out that any appeal could result in a negative outcome for you. If it emerges that your grade should have been lower than the one awarded, then your result will be downgraded accordingly!

Further help
BBC GCSE Bitesize: www.bbc.co.uk/schools/gcsebitesize
Buster Tests (GCSE Revision Tests): www.bustertests.co.uk
Examzone (a site hosted by Edexcel): www.examzone.co.uk
GCSE.com: www.gcse.com
Revision Notes (Revision and Course Notes): www.revision-notes.co.uk/GCSE
S-Cool! Revision: www.s-cool.co.uk
Stafford, Petrouchka *A–Z of Exam Survival*, Trotman.

End note: What next?

In this section you will:
> ◈ **find out a bit more about some of the options open to you after your Key Stage 4 qualifications.**

Compulsory schooling in this country ends at age 16. However, government policy now favours the idea of all young people staying in some form of learning post-16. This does not necessarily mean staying on at school. The main options are: school; a college of further education; or a training programme (which may be with a training provider or an employer).

In any case, once you've chosen your Key Stage 4 qualifications, it won't be long before you have to think about what to do afterwards. In fact, you may even have some thoughts in this direction already, not least if you have a particular career pathway in mind. Here are some of the options.

GCE A levels and AS levels

A levels remain the most widely known post-16 qualification. They are seen as the traditional gateway to higher education for the majority, although there are other excellent routes (BTEC Nationals, International Baccalaureate, etc.). A levels offer considerable flexibility of choice because of the way they are structured, with AS and A2 programmes. You can decide which subjects you would like to study and whether you want to complete a full A level or to study a subject for a year (and take an AS level) before deciding whether to study the second year and completing the A level by taking the A2 programme.

A level consists of two parts: the AS and the A2. The Advanced Subsidiary (AS) is a stand-alone qualification: it can be taken on its own and without progressing to the A2 stage (the second half of a full A level qualification). It consists of three units (assessed at the standard expected for a student halfway through an A level course). These units contribute 50% of the full A level qualification. Most units are assessed by examination, but some are assessed through coursework. In most A levels coursework accounts for 20–30% of the marks.

The AS tends to cover the less demanding material in an A level course, while the A2 covers the more demanding material. For example, in the A2 students might:

» specialise in an area they studied at AS
» extend their knowledge and understanding of the subject by studying new topics
» improve their skills further.

Also in the A2 students will combine knowledge, understanding and skills from across the A level course.

Applied A levels
'Applied' versions of the A level course are available in a small number of subjects:

» Art and Design
» Business Studies
» Engineering
» Health and Social Care
» ICT
» Leisure Studies
» Media
» Performing Arts
» Science
» Travel and Tourism.

Applied A levels are designed to develop your knowledge, skills and understanding in a broad vocational area. They are intended to equip students with up-to-date knowledge, skills and understanding of the sectors they represent. Learning is expected to be active, usually with some input from employers. Applied A levels are therefore an excellent preparation for further study or training.

Both A levels and Applied A levels are acceptable for entry into higher education. However, if you are planning to enter higher education on a particular course it is always important to check the entry requirements.

AEAs (Advanced Extension Awards)

In the case of some A level subject areas, there is an additional A level qualification available to more able students. If you are expecting to get A grades in your A levels you may want to consider taking an Advanced Extension Award (AEA), which requires a greater depth of understanding than A level.

AEAs are designed to challenge the most able A level students, ensuring that they are tested against standards comparable to the most demanding found in other countries. They are designed to be accessible to all able students, whatever their school or college and whichever qualification they are studying. They also help universities to differentiate between the most able candidates, particularly in subjects with a high proportion of A grades at A level or in those where competition for university places is particularly fierce.

The subjects in which the AEA is available include:

» Business Studies
» Economics
» English
» Geography
» History
» Latin
» Mathematics
» Modern Foreign Languages (French, German and Spanish)
» Psychology
» Religious Studies
» Science (Biology, Chemistry and Physics)
» Welsh
» Welsh as a Second Language.

International Baccalaureate (IB)

The International Baccalaureate Organisation offers a two-year programme of international education for students aged 16 to 19. The IB Diploma is a prestigious qualification and an excellent preparation for higher education study, and it is widely recognised by the world's leading universities.

Following the two-year curriculum of the IB Diploma programme, students are encouraged to:

» ask challenging questions
» learn how to learn

- develop a strong sense of their own identity and culture
- develop the ability to communicate with and understand people from other countries and cultures.

Retaking GCSEs

It is possible to retake GCSEs. This may be a good idea, but only if you have genuine reasons for thinking you can do better second time round. For example, you might feel that your progress through Key Stage 4 was hampered by illness or by a family trauma of some sort. Or that you really did not do enough work and will be better motivated if you do go for retakes. In this case especially, you might want to consider taking a mix of subjects, some in which you need better grades and one or more new subjects that might refresh your interest.

On the other hand, it might be an indication that GCSEs are not the right sort of qualification for you and that you would do better to consider an alternative learning programme, for example a BTEC or an Apprenticeship.

The awarding bodies do offer some English, Mathematics and Science syllabuses for examination in November. This can be very helpful for students who are ready to move on, but who need to improve their grade in one of these core subjects. Further details of the availability of November resits can be obtained from the awarding bodies.

Candidates wishing to repeat GCSE exams are able to carry forward their moderated coursework marks. The credit may be used only once and within a 12-month period following the initial issue of results.

BTEC qualifications

See also the entry on BTEC qualifications on page 24.

Post-16, BTEC offers a BTEC First (one-year course) and a BTEC National (two-year course).

The BTEC First is a level 2 qualification which can be used to help you get into training or employment, or to move into the next stage of study (which might be a BTEC Diploma, Applied A level, or other option).

BTEC Nationals are vocational qualifications that prepare students either for direct entry into employment or for progression to higher education. The qualification comes in three forms, all at NQF level 3: BTEC National Award; BTEC National Certificate; and BTEC National Diploma.

The BTEC Diploma can also be used to get into training or employment, but it is the equivalent to A levels, so it can also lead to higher education options.

OCR Nationals

OCR Nationals are available post-16, usually in FE colleges. See entry for OCR Nationals on page 25.

Further education

You may tend to think first about staying on at your school beyond 16 – if it has a sixth form. On the other hand you might find you have had enough of the school environment and going to a Further Education (FE) college would be a new and interesting challenge. Some FE colleges offer A level options with a range of vocational alternatives (including BTECs and NVQs), while others tend to specialise more in vocational qualifications. FE colleges have specialised vocational departments where you can do courses in areas like Catering, Engineering, Hair and Beauty, or Leisure and Tourism.

If you want to follow a particular career such as agriculture or horticulture you may want to attend a specialised college, one that runs only courses in a particular vocational area. Attending a specialised college could mean you have to travel a lot or need to live near the college during the week in term time.

To help you decide which institution to study at, FE colleges (like schools with sixth forms) produce prospectuses that tell you exactly what subjects and qualifications they can offer. They also hold open days which will give you the opportunity to find out more about the institution, talk to subject tutors and ask any questions you may have.

Apprenticeships

Apprenticeships give young people the opportunity to leave full-time education and take up on-the-job training. Doing an Apprenticeship means that you learn on the job: you study for a nationally recognised qualification and earn money while you learn. There are different types of Apprenticeship available, but they all lead to one or more of the following qualifications:

- National Vocational Qualifications (NVQs)
- Key Skills qualifications
- a technical qualification such as a BTEC or City and Guilds.

There are over 180 Apprenticeships available across more than 80 industrial sectors. They cover areas such as:

- Administration
- Agriculture
- Construction
- Customer Service, Retailing and Wholesaling
- Engineering
- Finance, Insurance and Real Estate
- Health and Beauty
- Manufacturing
- Media and Printing
- Recreation and Travel
- Transportation.

National Vocational Qualifications (NVQs)

In NVQs you learn mainly through practical, work-related tasks that are designed to help you develop the skills and knowledge to do a job effectively. NVQs normally feature plenty of work-based learning and most often include some study at work or college. You can also take an NVQ qualification at level 2 or 3 as part of an Apprenticeship.

There are over 1300 different NVQs. They are available in the vast majority of business sectors, including:

- business and management
- construction and property
- engineering
- food, catering and leisure services
- health and social care
- manufacturing, production and engineering
- sales, marketing and distribution
- sport and recreation

and are linked to specific jobs, e.g. hairdresser or plumber.

NVQs are based on national standards for various occupations. The standards say what a competent person in a job could be expected to do. As you progress through the course, you compare your skills and knowledge with these standards, so you can see what you need to do to meet the standards.

NVQs are designed to be taken at a pace that suits your needs, so there is no maximum time limit for the completion of an NVQ. However, it is most common for learners to take about a year to complete an NVQ at level 1 and 2, and around two years for an NVQ at level 3.

Completing an NVQ can lead to further training at the next NVQ level. You could go all the way to a level 5 NVQ and/or professional qualifications, usually in a related area. If you've studied an NVQ at level 3, you could also go on to a higher education course in a related vocational area.

How are NVQs taught and assessed?
NVQs are available at levels 1 to 5 on the National Qualifications Framework. They are assessed on practical assignments and a portfolio of evidence. Normally, a qualified assessor will observe you and question you about the real work you carry out in the workplace (or a realistic working environment). They will test your knowledge and understanding as well as your actual performance. Your assessor will sign off individual units within the NVQ when you have reached the required standard. The assessment will tell you whether you are considered to be 'competent' or 'not yet competent'.

Other vocational qualifications
There are many other vocational courses and qualifications, in areas such as art and design (e.g. Diploma in Foundation Studies) and working with children (e.g. CACHE Diploma). You can find out more about these and others via the websites listed below.

Straight into employment
It is possible to go straight into paid employment at 16+, but it is generally recommended that you do not take this option unless the employer is offering some form of accredited further training or learning. This might be an Apprenticeship, leading to an NVQ or a BTEC qualification. We are always hearing about a few entrepreneurs who have managed to carve out a very successful career without the benefit of formal qualifications, but this is probably getting harder – and there are usually more and better options available to you if you do have some qualifications as evidence of your knowledge, skills and understanding.

How to find out more
Apprenticeships: www.apprenticeships.org.uk
BTEC: www.edexcel.org.uk
CACHE Diploma: www.cache.org.uk
Careers Wales: www.careerswales.com

Connexions: www.connexions-direct.com
DCSF Qualifications for schools and colleges: www.dcsf.gov.uk/qualifications/
Diploma in Foundation Studies: www.edexcel.org.uk/quals/fad/
Edexcel: www.edexcel.org.uk
Education Maintenance Allowance: ema.direct.gov.uk/ema.html
International Baccalaureate: www.ibo.org
Learndirect: www.learndirect-advice.co.uk/findacourse/
NVQs: www.qca.org.uk/14-19/qualifications/
Student AS/A level guide (QCA): www.qca.org.uk
UK250 (links to FE college websites): www.uk250.co.uk/College/